To Grace,

With our b[...]

& gratitude for your encouragement.

14. August 2002

Sermons by the Lake

Yours sincerely,

Reginald Mallett

Sermons by the Lake

Inspiration at Junaluska

Reginald Mallett

Junaluska Resources
PROVIDENCE HOUSE PUBLISHERS
FRANKLIN, TENNESSEE

Printed in the United States of America

05   04   03   02   01   1   2   3   4   5

Library of Congress Catalog Card Number: 2001088958

ISBN: 1-57736-237-3

Cover design by Gary Bozeman
Cover photo by Pat Stewart

✝Junaluska Resources
▲ PROVIDENCE HOUSE PUBLISHERS
238 Seaboard Lane Franklin, Tennessee 37067
800-321-5692
www.providencehouse.com

To the United Methodist Assembly,
Lake Junaluska, North Carolina,
in gratitude and affection.

Contents

FOREWORD   ix

PREFACE   xi

1. God's Millionaires   1

2. Can You Hear the Pipes?   13

3. The Midday Sickness and Its Cure   25

4. Conflict in a Classroom   37

5. The Grace of Gratitude   51

6. Walk Tall   65

7. Tapestry, Window, or Door?   75

8. I Wonder What He Saw?   85

9. The Genuine Article   97

10. Providential Disturbance   109

11. God's Accounting   123

12. The Language of Love   135

NOTES   147

ABOUT THE AUTHOR   148

Foreword

✝

In the last thirty-five years, Dr. Reginald Mallett has preached over one hundred thought-provoking and life-changing sermons to an estimated 150,000 people at Lake Junaluska Assembly. During the summer of 2000 alone, he shared ten different homilies. To say that his preaching has touched thousands of lives for Christ at Lake Junaluska would be an understatement.

Sermons by the Lake is a collection of lessons preached by Dr. Mallett to different groups who have come to Lake Junaluska seeking renewal and spiritual refreshment. As you read this book, our prayer is that your life and actions will be touched anew by the transforming power of the gospel so eloquently communicated by Reginald Mallett. Without having heard Dr. Mallett or being present at Lake Junaluska, you can still be influenced by the unique Junaluska experience.

This is the first of many materials that will be made available through Junaluska Resources, an imprint of Providence House Publishers. Every year over fifty thousand people come to Lake Junaluska for workshops, seminars, retreats, entertainment, and worship. Our goal for the future is to capture the best of those events and make them available through print, compact discs, and the Internet.

Reginald Mallett has given us wonderful gifts through the years with his dynamic preaching. Now he has given us a more wonderful gift, this book of his sermons. Thank you, Dr. Mallett, for all the joy you continue to bring to God's children, challenging us all to lead lives exemplary of the disciples of Christ.

Joy T. Carr
Director of Ministry

Jimmy L. Carr
Executive Director

Southeastern Jurisdictional
Administrative Council

Preface

✝

Most of us have special places where we are acutely aware of God's presence. For me, as for many, Lake Junaluska, North Carolina, is such a place. The setting is magnificent. The peacefulness of the lake and the surrounding majestic mountains speak powerfully of their Creator. Many like us have been blessed by the lake's ministry. Time and again we have been thrilled to hear the lordship of Christ affirmed and the challenge to Christian commitment presented. Lake Junaluska has been a source of renewal and encouragement to my wife and me for over thirty-five years. To share in its ministry is a very rare privilege and my gratitude is inexpressible.

My special thanks are due to the Reverend Jimmy Carr, executive director of the Lake Junaluska Assembly. It was he who suggested that some of the sermons delivered there might be presented in a more permanent form, and this selection is the result. It is impossible to capture in print the settings in which the messages were presented. The beauty of Junaluska and the inspiration of worship provide a moving context for preaching. I hope, however, that a little of the sense of wonder and challenge which is the Junaluska experience might be reflected in these pages.

Someone in the crowd said to him,
"Teacher tell my brother
to divide the inheritance with me."
. . . [Jesus] said to them,
"Watch out! Be on your guard
against all kinds of greed;
a man's life does not consist
in the abundance of his possessions."

LUKE 12:13–15 (NIV)

Chapter One

God's Millionaires

August 2000

*I*t was Christmas morning. Our entire family was staying with us for the festive season and we were all in church for the traditional Christmas morning family service. We filled a whole pew. At one end sat my wife, Brenda, holding our youngest grandson, then just a toddler. I was at the other end looking across at my children and grand-children with gratitude and pride. It is a blissful heartwarming experience to be surrounded by one's nearest and dearest in church at any time but especially on Christmas Day. My mind soared to the heavens.

I was brought back to earth with a jolt! We were singing the hymn "Joy to the World." Brenda remained seated with little Martin on her lap. Suddenly a thought flashed through her mind. "Did I leave the pan on the stove?" She tried to shut it out but it returned with added urgency. For her, the serenity of the golden moment had fled. She found herself thinking "I don't remember taking the pan off the stove." The rest of us, unaware of her anxiety, continued singing. In her mind, however, a frightening possibility was swiftly becoming a certainty. She was now saying to herself, "I *know* I left the pan on the stove." Visions of the pan catching fire and our home in flames on Christmas morning filled her mind. She turned to our daughter standing beside her and whispered, "Pass a message to Dad. Tell him to go home and take the pan off the stove." The message was whispered along the row until it reached me. I glanced across and saw the worry on my wife's face and slipped out of church. I jumped in the car and drove like Jehu along the deserted Christmas morning roads to our home five miles away. (Jehu is a character in the Old Testament who is reported to have "driven furiously." He can be met most days on our roads!) As I raced I listened for the sirens of the fire engines on their way to rescue our house from destruction. I heard none. When I arrived at the house I could see no billowing smoke nor tongues of flame. There was no pan on the cooker. All was secure. My wife was mistaken!

I dashed back to the church. By that time the preacher was in the middle of an illustration in his sermon. I learned later that he was illustrating how, in the Incarnation, Jesus identified with our human situation. He told of a doctor who was called to examine a small boy at home. The six year old, scared of doctors, had hidden under the bed. In order to overcome the child's fear and gain his confidence the doctor had crawled under the bed alongside him. By the time I had resumed my seat the doctor was having a conversation with the young patient under the bed. I was puzzled; this was not the way I was taught to conduct a pediatric examination. On the way home I asked my wife "What on earth was that doctor doing under the bed?" She laughed and then told me the whole story. Because I heard only part, I had missed the point of what was being said.

It is an occupational hazard for us preachers that congregations do not always hear everything we say. Sometimes it is our fault; we have not been clear. Sometimes the problem lies with the hearer. Many come to worship with minds burdened by all kinds of things. For one it may be a worry about a close member of the family. For another it may be the dread of a doctor's appointment. For another it may be concern about mounting bills. The longer I preach, the more my heart goes out to my hearers, many of whom face an uphill struggle every day and who are little short of heroic.

It is Luke who tells us about this man who interrupted Jesus. The Master had been speaking about God's providential care that even reaches out to sparrows and counts the hairs of our heads. Just as I had missed the point of the preacher's Christmas morning sermon illustration because I heard only part of it, so this man in the gospel story hearing only part of what Jesus was saying about God's providential care, misunderstands. He blurts out *"Teacher tell my brother to divide the family inheritance with me."* We need to do a little digging here to find out why he would make such a spectacle of himself in front of a crowd of people.

Behind this man's abrupt interruption lies a family sorrow. His father had died. Perhaps the bereavement was recent because the settlement was still a burning issue in his mind. Jewish law was very precise about inheritance. It decreed that on the death of a father, his property was to be divided equally between each of his sons with the exception of the eldest who was to receive a double portion. This sounds like unfair favoritism but it was, in fact, a wise provision. Upon the shoulders of the oldest son fell the responsibility of caring for his widowed mother. He was also expected to look after any unmarried sisters and provide their dowries when they married. Because of these extra commitments, the Law allowed additional resources.

Perhaps in this case, however, none of these circumstances applied. Perhaps there was no widowed mother to look after. Perhaps there were no unmarried sisters. If this were so, then it did not seem fair for one son to receive twice as much as the other. The issue is burning in this man's soul. He is rankled and only half listening to Jesus. He is not bearing a grief: he is nursing a grievance. We can imagine the thoughts going through his mind. "What was it the preacher just said? 'Are not five sparrows sold for two pennies? Yet not one of them is forgotten by God . . . you are worth more than many sparrows.' He is talking about worth and value. Pennies and sparrows. If there is such a providence as this, can I not call it to my aid? What about my inheritance?" Forgetting everything else that Jesus has been saying, and taking this one thing completely out of context, he blurts out: "Teacher, speak to my brother to divide the inheritance between us."

Jesus takes this domestic squabble and gives it an eternal dimension. "Life," He said "does not consist in possessions." He reminds us that ultimately all the big issues in our lives are theological.

WHAT JESUS SAID IS CLEAR

Years ago I saw an old black-and-white film entitled *Whistle Down The Wind*. In the film, some children have found a vagrant in a barn. For various reasons they are convinced that this homeless, wandering man is Jesus. They have a sick kitten about which they are worried. With childlike trust they take it to the vagrant expecting him to make it well. The kitten dies. Now they begin to ask profound questions. "Why do people become ill? Why do people die? Why did our kitten die? What does dying mean?" The children can think of only one person in the village who could supply answers to questions such as these. That person is the vicar, the minister of the local parish church.

The children go round to the vicarage and knock on the door. They are ushered into the presence of the vicar who is having afternoon tea as they enter. Being children, there were no preliminary pleasantries, no prevarication. They come straight to the point with their questions.

"Why do people become ill? Why do people die? Why did our kitten die?" The vicar, managing to beam in a patronizing way, puts down his cup and saucer and responds with correct orthodox answers straight from a textbook of systematic theology. He releases a cloud of nice, rounded religious words. When he has finished he sits back and pours himself another cup of tea. He is purring with self-satisfaction over a job well done. The children are mystified. Realizing their interview is over, they walk slowly to the door. One little boy turns to the girl who is the leader of the band and whispers quite loudly, "He doesn't know either, does he?"

Jesus did not hide behind pretentious or obscure words. There is nothing vague about the answer he gives to this disturbed man. With love and gentleness he looks into his troubled face and says, "I am not talking about *things*, I am after much bigger game. I am talking about *life*. One day the farm will have gone. Everything you or your brother now covet will have passed away. The only thing that will last is *life* when you have it in its fullness. And *life* does not consist in possessions." The disgruntled man is being offered heaven and he does not realize it. He is more interested in a piece of property. Recognizing his problem, Jesus tells a story about a successful farmer.

Like most preachers, I have a sermon about this farmer. It is a very popular theme for harvest festivals. Like most preachers, I suspect, I have been unfair to him. In the story, Jesus does not indicate that this man has broken any law. There is nothing here about graft or theft, nor is there any suggestion that employees have been ill treated. It is not to be supposed that he has acquired any of his goods by underhand methods. Thanks to his sweat and industry and with the blessing of sun, soil, and rain he has become moderately wealthy. He is precisely the kind of person we admire. There would be no difficulty in delivering a glowing eulogy at his funeral. He has been careful and frugal. He has not been unjust. He has made wise provision for his retirement so that he would not be a burden on his family. He is not looking for a handout from anyone. Our conclusion would be "Well done!"

God's verdict is very different. But notice that Jesus is not saying here that there is anything wrong with possessions wisely used. God's verdict is not "You wicked man!" It is "You fool!" He is a fool because he had not realized the impermanence of material things, that they do not amount to *life.*

We live in a world of things. We surround ourselves with things. We have more things than any other generation that has ever lived. The commercials on television are filled with news about things. Cars, houses, exotic vacations, computers, videos—the list is endless. And there is the unspoken assertion lying behind this preoccupation with things that the secret of life is in getting more. What a tragedy if the epitaph for our age were to be "They had everything to live *with* but nothing to live *for.*" *Beware of covetousness. Life does not consist in the abundance of the things we possess.* This word of Jesus is clear.

WHAT JESUS SAID IS PERSONAL

The man who interrupted Jesus felt aggrieved. He believed he had a problem and what he wanted was not a sermon but action. His problem was clear to him; it was his

brother. Most of us are like him. Our problems and difficulties are equally clear—our brother, our sister, our
colleague at work, our son, our daughter, the members of
the church. We want someone to come and deal with them;
"Lord, speak to my brother."

When I was eighteen years of age I was the secretary of
a large church youth club. We had over a hundred members
and it was probably the most impressive gathering of
young people in our town. We attended Sunday evening
service in a group. We met each Saturday for discussions
and debates and each Wednesday for various types of
indoor games. Perhaps today such activities might seem
tame. We thought we were having a great time.

In the summer of that year a group of young
evangelists from a Methodist Bible college held a mission
for ten days at a small church on the outskirts of our town.
Out of curiosity three of us attended the Monday evening
service. There was only a handful of people present. They
were all advanced in years and there was no visible
response to the preacher's pleading invitation. We were
impressed by the sincerity of these earnest young men and
afterwards we stayed to have a word with them. I was
appointed spokesman. I approached their leader, Clive,
and said, "Would you like to come to speak at our youth
club next Saturday night?" I proudly added, "We can
guarantee at least a hundred young people in your
audience." I thought Clive would be eager to seize such a
marvelous opportunity. I will never forget his response.
He looked me straight in the eyes and said, "What does
Jesus Christ mean to you?"

I was tongue-tied and so were my two companions. He
had clearly missed the point. We were talking about the
youth club. We were offering him and his colleagues an

opportunity of preaching to a large group of able young people. I assumed I had not made myself clear, and so I repeated the invitation. "You had fewer than twenty in your congregation this evening," I said. "We can guarantee over one hundred young people next Saturday." Again he looked at the three of us and, with a winsome smile, said "But what does Jesus Christ mean to you?"

As a result of his direct penetrating words that evening in June, the three of us gave our lives to Christ. Later those evangelists did come to the youth club and we saw numbers of our friends make the same step of faith. On that Monday evening, however, when I said "Speak to our youth club," Clive spoke directly to me and said "First, what about your walk with God?"

We had started off like the man in the gospel story. He came to Jesus and said "Speak to my brother." We are always pointing at someone else and our plea is "Lord, speak to my children, speak to my neighbors, speak to those I work with, speak to my minister." Jesus, however, challenges us just as he challenged this man who interrupted him in the gospel story. "Take another look," He says, "you do not *have* a problem, you *are* a problem." Our deepest need does not lie with our brother, it does not lie in rearranging the family inheritance or the furniture of our lives. Our deepest need lies in focusing on the true meaning of life. It is a personal word. "It's not my mother, it's not my brother, it's me O Lord. . . ."

WHAT JESUS SAID IS SAVING

In *Stories Jesus Still Tells*, John Claypool relates something which Samuel Miller said in one of his lectures. Miller, the dean of the divinity school at Harvard University for many years, tells of being in Munich in 1931 when German culture was flourishing. One night he went to the Bavarian National Opera House to see one of the last of what he called "The Metaphysical Clowns," a man named Karl Valentino. Dressed like a clown and doing clownlike pantomimes, Valentino conveyed profound truths.

The mime began with a stage that was bare except for one circle of light. The clown entered that circle and began to search very diligently for something he had lost. After a time, a policeman came up. "Have you lost something?" he asked. "The key to my house," replied the clown. "If I can't find it, I can't go home tonight." With that the policeman joined in the search with great intensity. Finally he asked, "Are you sure you lost it here?" "Oh, I didn't lose it here, I lost it over there," said the clown pointing to a darkened part of the stage. "Then why on earth are you looking here?" the policeman asked. "Because there's no light over there," the clown replied.

Such an exchange may seem terribly foolish on a superficial level, but beneath the action, Miller saw a profound symbol of human futility. To look for something where it cannot be found is the ultimate formula for disappointment. To search for *life* by getting *things* is a quest destined to fail abysmally.

Not having possessions can be a great trial. Poverty is a harsh teacher and those of us who were brought up poor remember its lessons. I attended a privileged fee-paying boys' school having gained a free scholarship by competitive examination. On our first day at the school we were each assigned to one of four "houses" for sporting activities. My house was "Tyldesley" and we were told we had to wear green soccer shirts on the playing field. I reported this to my mother. She could not afford to buy one, but she did her best.

She took an old white shirt and dyed it green. Unfortunately, it was a different green than the shirts the other boys wore. Anyone can understand how important that would be to a ten year old. I used to dread Friday afternoons when the timetable decreed that we were to play soccer. Each week I would try to find some excuse such as a sprained ankle, a bruised knee, or a migraine headache to avoid going out on the soccer field wearing that oddly colored shirt.

The strange thing, however, is that I did not grow up feeling poor. My dear mother with her firm Baptist background and her simple faith would say again and again "Remember, son, it is not what you *have* but what you *are* that counts." And that message got through to me. "Life does not consist in the abundance of possessions."

This is a saving word for those who have ears to hear. There is nothing wrong with possessions rightly used as long as we understand that they do not provide the key to life. One day they will all pass from us. What we are left with is what we truly are. And when we give ourselves to Christ we become rich with a deeper wealth than can be derived just from things. We become rich towards God which means finding the true meaning of life. To discover this is to experience salvation. This word of Jesus is not only clear and personal—it is saving.

A young, ambitious student was having a conversation with the great evangelist Dwight L. Moody. "What are your plans?" Moody asked. "I plan to graduate with honors," the young man replied. "What then?" asked Moody. "I plan to get a good position in a company and work my way to a partnership," he said. "What then?" asked Moody. "Well, I hope to make my fortune, marry, and have a family." "What then?" asked Moody. "I hope I will make enough money for me to retire comfortably." "What then?" persisted Moody. "I suppose I will live on my resources and grow old gracefully." "What then?" came the remorseless question. The young man faltered. "Well I suppose I will die," he said softly. "What _then?_" said the evangelist with gentle earnestness, "What then? What then?" One day the Angel of Death comes calling. Then all our things, all our delightful, desirable things for which we have sacrificed so much, are taken from us. What we _are_, however, travels with us into the realm of light.

This word of Jesus is clear; each of us can understand it. It is personal. Above all, it is saving if we have the wisdom to lay hold upon its message. Have you discovered the secret of _life?_ Have you discovered that _life_ does not lie in what you _have_ but in what you _are?_ If what you are is from Christ, then happy are you. Congratulations! You are one of God's millionaires. You are Christ's. And Christ is God's.

✝

*. . . in hope that the creation itself
will be liberated from its bondage to decay
and brought into the glorious freedom
of the children of God.*

ROMANS 8:21 (NIV)

Chapter Two

Can You Hear the Pipes?

August 2000

uring my years in medical family practice I visited many patients in their homes. There was nothing unusual about that; house calls are routine for doctors in England. One visit, however, stands out in my mind.

Alex was a patient with a serious heart condition. I made calls to his home on a regular basis and they were always delightful experiences. A widower for a number of years, he had a remarkably broad range of interests. He was widely read. He had travelled extensively. Above all he loved music. On this particular afternoon he mentioned that he played the violin. He then went across to a corner cabinet and opened it to reveal a shelf on which four violins were neatly arranged on stands. Underneath them on the floor of the cabinet was a set of bagpipes.

Those bagpipes fascinated me. I could not resist telling him the story which the distinguished conductor Sir Thomas Beecham used to tell. After conducting a concert on one occasion, Beecham was approached by a lady who had a twelve-year-old son whom she considered a budding genius. The boy had announced to his doting mother that he wished to take up a musical instrument. "Sir Thomas," she said, "my son intends to learn a musical instrument and I would like your advice. Can you recommend an instrument which will not be too painful on our ears while he is going through the learning stage?" Without any hesitation Beecham replied "Madam, I would unreservedly recommend the bagpipes. They sound just as bad when they are played well as when they are played badly!"

My patient Alex laughed. Fortunately, he was not a Scot. Then he became rather wistful. He smiled and said, "Yes, I can imagine Beecham saying that. But, you know," then he paused and almost with a caress picked up the bagpipes which he cradled in his arms before continuing, "for me there is no sound in all the world like the sound of the pipes." He then went on to explain.

During World War II, like thousands of others, I was a prisoner in Burma. Those days were awful and they seemed endless. Some of my friends in our camp died and most of us were often very ill. There was a lot of cruelty and little food, but I won't bore you with details, they are well known. One day late in the war—we had lost track of dates—one of my friends, Sandy, a Welshman from somewhere near Cardiff called us over and pointed out that something was afoot. The Japanese guards were cleaning out the camp commandant's wooden office. They were bringing out boxes of papers and burning them. Next day several trucks drew up and all the guards climbed aboard. The camp commandant took his seat in the first truck and they drove off. We prisoners were left standing in the compound with the gates wide open. It was weird. There were no noises, no shouts or commands, just an eerie silence broken only by the noises of the birds and insects in the jungle beyond the wire. We all wondered what was going on. Was this some cruel trick?

We stood around for about two hours in the hot sun sensing that something was about to happen. Suddenly our camp medical officer shouted "Hush!" He strained his ears. "Listen!" he cried, "Can you hear it?" "Hear what?" someone asked. "Why, the pipes," said the Scottish doctor. "Can you hear the pipes?" We all thought that he had finally lost his mind—he had worked harder than anyone trying to keep us all alive. But he was so insistent that we all listened intently. One by one we heard it too. At first it was very faint but quite unmistakable. It was a sound which a Scot such as our medical officer would immediately recognize. It was the skirl of bagpipes. The sound grew louder and round a bend in the dirt road leading to the camp came one of the most wonderful sights in all the world. It was a solitary piper! Behind him came a jeep carrying a senior British officer followed by marching Scottish infantry. We gathered round the officer and he stood to address us. "The enemy has gone," he said. "Your imprisonment is over. You are all free men. Transport and supplies are on their way so that you chaps can start your journey home. You've done your share. We're not finished yet so we have to press on. God bless you all." He gave a command, the piper started up again and the jeep slowly moved on.

Alex looked down at the bagpipes he was holding and said very softly and with deep emotion "You know, doctor, ever since that day, whenever I hear the sound of the pipes, I have a thrilling sense of freedom."

As I think of Alex's story, I am reminded that the message of salvation is for the Christian believer the sound of the pipes. In Paul's words, the gospel of Christ brings with it adoption into God's family and "the glorious freedom of the children of God" (Rom. 8:21).

THE PIPES PROCLAIM FREEDOM FROM FEAR

Fear! Even the word itself seems to send a shiver down our spines. Perhaps that is why it is used so much by newspaper editors. Bravado might prompt some to say "What in the world have I to be afraid of?" But they would not have to think long before their bluff would be called. There is fear of that doctor's appointment for one thing. Then there is fear about job uncertainty. "Downsizing" is just a fancy word to dress up the fact that the company plans to get rid of staff that might include one of us. "Being let go" is just as painful as "getting fired." Words don't soften the blow. For parents there are fears about the children, innocent hostages to fortune. Teenagers bring to their parents many blessings but they also bring a burden of fear—the automobile on the busy highway, the influence of peers, the terrible temptations of the drug culture. What in the world have I to be afraid of? Plenty!

This gets all complicated by our wrong ideas about God. It is amazing how many carry around a distorted version of the Christian faith. I want to call this version "folk religion" because it is so often buried deep beneath our consciousness. It is a vague idea of God standing in the shadows with a big stick waiting for us to step out of line. When we do, that stick falls. Have we not heard good, loving, and sincere men and women respond to some calamity by saying "Why did God let it happen to me? What did I do to deserve such a thing?" Even some who try to bring comfort compound the problem. After some awful, painful event they say "It's God's will." As though the Author of all that is good and joyful would deliberately inflict sickness or anguish. The result is that instead of finding comfort and strength in their Christian faith, many in distress find their fears reinforced.

My friend Alex and his companions never knew a day free from fear since the moment they were taken prisoners. Fear was their constant companion. There was the fear of their captors and the things they did. There was the fear of punishment for minor infractions of petty camp rules. There was fear of hunger, fear of the dreadful diseases that were rampant, fear that they would never see their loved ones again. A lonely unmarked grave in an unknown part of a foreign country seemed the only prospect in view. But when they heard the sound of the pipes, fear fled and hope came in its place.

The men and women to whom the Apostle Paul was writing knew all about fear. There were more slaves than free men in the Roman Empire and many of them were Christians. They suffered similar privations, indignities, and violations as those men in the prison camp. They knew all the fears we experience today and more besides. For them the message of salvation, of being adopted into the family of God, was like the sound of the pipes to my friend Alex. It meant freedom from fear and the birth of hope. Now they knew that God in Christ was not against them but on their side.

When I was very young I held my father in awe. If I wanted any favors then I would go to my mother. She acted as the go-between. One Sunday night I experienced a revelation about his nature that changed my whole perception and banished my fear. I was about seven years old. Dad took me to evening service at the parish church because my older brother who was in the choir was to sing a solo. Mother stayed at home to look after my two younger brothers. I sat in that historic stone church with its high polished mahogany pews struggling to remain interested until my brother had sung. Then, like a normal seven year old I became utterly bored and began to feel sleepy. I gazed at the soaring gothic arches and the stained-glass windows. The service from the old prayer book seemed to go on forever. Finally the rector mounted the steps to the large stone pulpit and began his sermon. He had a remarkably soft, soothing voice. It was a special gift for any insomniac! It was able to coax the most alert into a gentle slumber. That evening I was fighting to stay awake—and losing the battle. My head nodded and then it nodded again, this time a little lower. Sleep was beckoning. At that moment I noticed my father's right hand move. I cringed expecting a slap to wake me up. Instead I found his powerful arm come round my shoulder as he gently pulled me down to rest my head on his lap so that I could sleep in comfort.

How many think of God as the One with the big stick? They cringe waiting for the slap rather than joyfully anticipating an enfolding embrace. Despite what we sing and say, many of us have not truly received the good news that God has been revealed as love. It is time for us to claim our right to the glorious freedom of the children of God. It is time for us to receive the assurance that we are held firm in the heart of the Holy One. Here is the promise of freedom from fear.

Listen! Can you hear the pipes?

THE PIPES PROCLAIM FREEDOM FROM ISOLATION

A child stands isolated, alone outside the school; all the others have friends, but he doesn't. A rebellious teenager simmers in her room resenting the reasonable rules of the house, isolated in the sullen state of war she has declared on the rest of the family. A woman struggles to prepare a meal for her three rowdy children. It is now months since her husband has walked out and she feels isolated having no one with whom she can share her problems. A man sits in a cold empty room at the end of the day, gazing at the television screen but not seeing anything in particular. He has felt isolated since his relationship broke up. An elderly woman lifts a cup to her mouth and spills the contents because of an uncontrollable tremor in her hands; she wonders what is to become of her, having no family and realizing she is unable to look after herself any longer. The experts tell us that the elderly dread isolation and loneliness as much as disease and death.

Has the good news which Christ brings anything to say to isolated people such as these?

Let's go back to Alex's story. He said that when he and his companions heard the sound of the pipes they knew that the end of their isolation was in sight. Soon he and his comrades, who had been separated from everything they cherished, would be surrounded with love once again. Transport was on its way to take them back to their homes and their families. The sound of the pipes promised glorious reunion.

The good news of the Gospel is that through the saving work of Christ we can all become members of the family of God. We can become members one of another. We can become part of the caring community in which hurts, joys, and burdens are all shared. Fanciful? No! The early church silenced the slanders of its traducers by its tender compassionate care. Read the early chapters of the Acts of the Apostles. From that record it can be seen why an astonished unbelieving world exclaimed "See how these Christians love one another!" Isolation ought to be unknown within the family of God.

As a schoolboy during the Second World War, I can remember my parents and their friends talking about how isolated we were when France capitulated to the Nazis. It was about this time that I moved to a new all boys' school. Each day began with a brief act of worship—a hymn, a Bible reading, and a prayer. This was compulsory and all pupils and teachers attended. Before we were dismissed to our classes the headmaster would give out any important notices. One day he dismissed the rest of the assembly but ordered those of us in the first year to remain behind. We naturally wondered what we had done wrong. The headmaster's stern countenance could make even the purest innocent feel guilty of some unconscious misdemeanor! Fortunately, on this occasion, all was benign. He held up two sheets of paper. "I have here," he announced, "the names and addresses of school children who live in the United States of America. They would like to correspond with pupils of similar age who live here. I will pin the lists on the notice board outside my study. If you are interested, make a note of one of the names and addresses and then cross it off so that two of you are not writing to the same person." He then walked out of the hall.

After a brief pause there was a stampede for the headmaster's notice board. As I joined the crowd I heard a howl of anguish from those who had arrived first. They had made the discovery that all the potential correspondents *were girls*—and we had not reached the age when that would be a powerful attraction! Worse, they all lived in one of those strange places in the New World we had never heard of. We had hoped for one of the exciting places we encountered in movies such as New York, Chicago, or Los Angeles. Instead these girls lived in a place called Seattle. (Knowing no better we all pronounced it See-tle.)

I took down a name and an address. I wrote four letters over the next few months to a girl called Dorothy who lived in See-tle. She even sent me a box of chocolates before the correspondence petered out. I often wondered where See-tle was. It was years later that I discovered it to be a very famous American city. Recently the actor Tom Hanks was featured in a film called *Sleepless in See-tle*. Oh, of course, I know now that it is pronounced Se-atle but to a ten-year-old English schoolboy that does not seem a natural way of interpreting the spelling of that city's name!

Those letters—and my experience could be multiplied by thousands all over the country—did something very significant. The reason why important and busy people on both sides of the Atlantic fostered the pen pal exchange program was to make us realize that we were not as isolated as we thought. Dorothy said that in her school they were talking about Britain every day. They heard about our air raids. They heard about our food shortage. They heard about Winston Churchill who was rallying the nation. It was a subtle comfort to be reminded that we were not alone.

Deep down, we all dread isolation. Ernest Hemingway in one of his stories tells of a Spanish father who wanted to be reconciled with his son who had run away to Madrid. The remorseful father took out an ad in the *El Liberal* newspaper. "Paco meet me at the Hotel Montana, Noon Tuesday. All is forgiven, Papa." Now Paco is a common name in Spain. When the father arrived in the square at the appointed time on the Tuesday he found eight hundred young men named Paco waiting for their fathers! They were weary of isolation.

When we become members of the family of God we experience the glorious freedom which is the right of his children. This means freedom from isolation. There is a new sense of belonging to a family which embraces all places and all ages. Has that experience come to you?

Listen! Can you hear the pipes?

THE PIPES PROCLAIM THE FREEDOM TO GO HOME

Out there in the Burmese jungle those men were a long way from the hills and meadows of their native England. But the pipes brought a glorious message of hope. Although prisoners, they did not belong in the jungle. They had a home and soon they would be on their way. The journey would take weeks, but *they were going home.*

The gospel announces our true address. That address is not the jungle where we are imprisoned. It is not the habit that has gripped us. It is not the broken relationship in our home that darkens every day. It is not the feeling of bitterness when we consider what others have done to us. Our true address is heaven. We are potential children of the loving God who weeps when we lose our way.

Perhaps the most loved figure in Methodism in the part of England where I grew up was a minister named John Henry Sanders. He was over eighty years of age when I first met him. He was a small, slightly built man with beautiful white hair and white moustache. At the end of the area conference at which I was unanimously recommended for the ministry, this dear man of God took me at one side. He put his arm on my shoulder and in his charming Cornish accent said, "Reg, my dear boy, my daughter wants me to move to her house so that she can look after me. I haven't room for all my books. Would you like to come and take some off my hands?" What an opportunity! "Yes please, Mr. Sanders," I said, "I would love to have some of your books." "Splendid!" he exclaimed. "Come round on Tuesday evening at 7 o'clock."

The following Tuesday I rode the bus to his daughter's home in Lower Walton taking with me a briefcase in which to carry the books. I was punctual; Mr. Sanders was renowned for his precise habits. He opened the door and invited me in. We chatted a while although I was eager to get round to the books. The time duly arrived. Beckoning me to follow him he led me out of the house and to the garage at the side. He opened the garage door and I could not restrain a gasp of astonishment. From floor to ceiling, from door to rear wall, the entire garage was packed with hundreds upon hundreds of books. The elderly minister looked at my little briefcase and then at the mountain of books before us. He stroked his moustache and with a mischievous twinkle in his eye he said affectionately "O ye of little faith!"

I subsequently made several visits to that garage! Most of the books this scholarly minister gave me have now been passed on to other younger ministers. Amongst the books I have kept for sentimental reasons is a collection of sermons by James Black, a great Scottish preacher of a previous day. In the volume is one sermon that bears an arresting title. Black tells his readers that it was given to him by a friend who had taken it from an inscription on a tombstone. "He was born a man and died a grocer." The title generates a host of ideas. Of course the calling to be a grocer, like most of life's callings, can be noble. But if the whole of what we *are* can be summed up in terms of what we *do* then something has gone wrong. We have lost our way. We are called to be more than the work in which we are engaged. We are called to be children of God with the unique privilege of finally sharing the glories and the joys of heaven. We are given the right, the freedom, to travel home to God.

The wonder of the gospel is that God has not been content to sit back and wait until we arrive. Most of us at some point lose our way. In Christ, God has come searching for us and guides our wandering footsteps home. Not only are we given the freedom to come home, we are also provided through the guidance of the Spirit with the inner transport to arrive safely there.

For Alex, since his Burma days, the sound of the pipes brought a thrilling sense of freedom. But he had an even more wonderful experience. You see, he had heard another set of pipes which heralded the glorious freedom of the children of God. He had heard the music of the gospel of Christ and had responded to it. When eventually he gently slipped away to glory I know it was that celestial music which gave him most joy. It sang to his soul of the freedom from fear, freedom from isolation, and the freedom to go home to heaven.

Listen! O listen! Can *you* hear the pipes?

You will not fear the terror of the night
or the arrow that flies by day,
or the pestilence that stalks in darkness
or the destruction that wastes at noonday.

PSALM 91:5–6 (NRSV)

Chapter Three

The Midday Sickness and Its Cure

August 2000

When I was seven years old, it was my great good fortune to come under the influence of a remarkable woman. For three of the most formative years of my life, Miss Boardman was my schoolteacher. At the age of ten I moved to another school, and she passed out of my life. Years later I tried to trace her but without success. Her Christian influence has, however, proved to be an enduring legacy through which my life has been immeasurably enriched. I thank God for Christian schoolteachers!

In those days, schoolteachers spent the first hour of each Monday morning dealing with a variety of administrative duties. During that time Miss Boardman made sure that we children were profitably occupied. On arriving we would find a Psalm written in chalk on the blackboard. We knew what was expected of us. We were to memorize it. The first pupil to recite it correctly was rewarded with a penny. How I bless Miss Boardman for those "Monday Morning Penny Psalms" that I still recall. Psalm 91 earned me my very first penny.

As I memorized it, I found comfort in the promise about the terror of the night. Like most children I was scared of the dark. Such a fear is instinctive. Despite my mother's patient reassurance, the dark bedroom seemed a threatening place.

Every creak and groan in our old home brought a host of terrors. Every shadow seemed sinister. The friendly darkened passages became, in my imagination, the lair of ghosts, scary animals, and make-believe strangers. I was glad to greet the morning light! I could also understand the psalmist's assurance of protection from arrows that flew by day. I had been to the movie theatre and seen Westerns. I knew about arrows. But the rest of the text was lost on me. Who cared about *"The destruction that wastes at noonday"*? Certainly not I!

With maturity I have to come to see that life's noonday is a most dangerous time. By then our major decisions have been made. We have already faced the challenges of education. The question of what work we are to do has been settled. We have made up our minds which church we will attend, the person with whom we are going to spend our lives, and where we are going to live. These big issues are behind us. It is at this point in our journey that we are tempted to sit back and let down our guard. At night we are vigilant. We post sentries and charge them to be alert. But at noonday we relax and say to ourselves "You can afford to eat, drink, and be merry." We take a spiritual and sometimes moral *siesta*.

The classic biblical example is King David. As a young man he was spurred on by his dreams. He knew the terror by night as he hid from his enemies in the cave of Adullam. He knew the spiritual rapture when Samuel anointed him with holy oil and declared that one day he would be king. In the morning of his life he was ready to do exploits for God and he sang the song of faith. Then he reached noonday. He had arrived. His major battles were over. Jerusalem was secured as the capital and he was installed as king. He had achieved his objectives. His dreams were fulfilled. That was the moment when he fell and we all know the story of Bathsheba and the murder of Uriah the Hittite.

King David is not alone. There comes a spiritual noonday for all of us and with it a destruction that can lay waste the soul. It is insidious in its onset but the battle is more than half won when we recognize how the disease works. What are the points of weakness in our lives where this destruction strikes? What are the symptoms and what is the cure?

The First Symptom—Hurry

We live in a world of hurry. Some years ago my wife and I were taken to a cheerful restaurant in an American town. We were led to our table by a delightful young man. Then, to our surprise, before menus were provided, glasses of water brought, napkins and cutlery laid, he produced a stop clock, started it, and placed it before us. He explained that it was the proud boast of that particular restaurant that if the meal were not served in ten minutes it was free! The meal arrived with just thirty seconds to spare! The speed of the service was the secret of the restaurant's success.

About twenty years ago I was standing by a carousel at London's Gatwick airport waiting for our luggage. I cannot think of a more depressing experience than getting off a transatlantic flight at 6:30 A.M. on a November morning having come from the sunshine of Florida. I was shivering and half asleep. Standing beside me was a most friendly American who was at least twenty years my senior. He was bounding with energy and did not give the slightest impression of having travelled through the night. It was quite intimidating, and I felt most inadequate.

As we waited, he told me that he had recently retired for the third time. He went on to explain that he had enjoyed three careers building up three different companies and very recently he had decided it was time to take things easy. Then he added "Mind you, every time I come to this country I feel like starting up again." "Doing what?" I asked. "Fast foods," he answered. "There's such an opportunity here in Europe." "No," I grunted. "That won't work here. Fast convenience food is just not British. As for the rest of Europe, I can't see the French, the Germans, or the Italians going for it either." He smiled. "We'll see," he said.

We *have* seen, and I could not have been more wrong! Wherever we go in Britain or across the channel on the European mainland, we find Kentucky Fried Chicken, McDonalds, Pizza Hut, Burger King, and lots of others. Fast food has arrived, and we Europeans love it as much as our American cousins. Hurry has overtaken us all.

Years ago a young Londoner was entertaining a student from the Indian subcontinent. Travelling on London's subway system—The Tube—they had to change trains to one on the Bakerloo line. Now the Bakerloo line had a *two minute* service. As they hurried through a labyrinth of escalators and passages there came the rumble of an approaching train. The young Englishman seized his guest and whirled him at a giddy rate through the remaining corridors onto the platform, where they hurled themselves through the closing doors of the train. They lay breathless and helpless for a long time, as the train roared on its way. When the young host could speak he gasped out triumphantly: "We've just saved two minutes." To which the bewildered visitor panted in reply: "What are you going to do with them?"

There is a spiritual dimension to the hurry that has overtaken this frenzied generation. God is in danger of being pushed out. We are too hurried for the whisper of heaven to be heard. Oh, I am not talking of being *busy*. Certainly let us live busy lives, full of purpose, service, worship, laughter, conversation, and fellowship. But we must beware of hurry. It is a symptom of the midday sickness. Hurry is not so much what we *do* as what we *are*. It is a frame of mind. Long ago the medieval mystic Thomas à Kempis said, "The humble in spirit dwell in a multitude of peace."

How do we prevent hurry from taking over our lives? How do we escape the midday sickness?

When I was eighteen I was led to Christ and introduced to a simple chorus. Its profound truth becomes more clear to me with each passing year.

Turn your eyes upon Jesus,
Look full in His wonderful face,
And the things of earth will grow strangely dim
In the light of His glory and grace.

As a cure for the midday sickness, I have a prescription to offer. Build into your day two or three brief pauses when you can retreat into your inner self. There quietly whisper these words and reflect on the humility and the glory of the Savior. This prescription does not require much time. It is not a matter of hours or even minutes. I am speaking of *transcendental moments* that have transforming power. I believe these moments will prove an antidote for this symptom of hurry and confer the grace, in the midst of busy lives, with which to dwell in that multitude of peace.

THE SECOND SYMPTOM—INFLEXIBILITY

On their sixth birthdays, we bought a book of poems for each of our children. The author was A. A. Milne, the creator of Winnie the Pooh. Our children would read them through again and again until they knew them by heart. We would hear them lying in bed at night reciting their favorites. Number one in their affection was the poem that gave the book its title, "Now We Are Six":

When I was one I had just begun.
When I was two I was nearly new.
When I was three I was hardly me.
When I was four, I was not much more.
When I was five I was just alive.
But now I am six. I'm as clever as clever.
So I think I'll be six now for ever and ever.[1]

This is the story of many of us when we reach our midday. We feel that we have no more growing to do. We want to stay where we are forever—even in our understanding of God.

You are perhaps familiar with the little girl who was having a deep theological discussion with her older brother. He was ten years old and therefore very wise. She asked him where God was. He said that God was everywhere. This puzzled her and so at breakfast next morning she took the matter to the highest possible authority, her father. He was a preacher and therefore obviously the fount of all wisdom concerning God. "Daddy," she said, "David says that God is everywhere. Is that true?" Her father nodded. "Does that mean that God is in this town and in this house?" "Yes," her father answered. "Does that mean God is in this room?" she said, becoming quite animated. Her father, thinking that his daughter was making a tremendous spiritual discovery, said "Yes, Katie, God is in this room." "Does that mean that God is here at this table?" she demanded. Again her father nodded. Then, holding up the little cup in which she normally placed her boiled egg she asked, "Does that mean that God is in this empty egg cup?" Puzzled at this strange turn of the discussion he said, "Well yes, Katie, God is everywhere so He must be in that egg cup." Katie clapped her hand on the egg cup and cried in triumph "Then I've got Him!"

In the morning of our walk with God, at the start of our spiritual journey, we were sensitive to the Spirit's leading. With childlike wonder and open mind we marvelled at the immensity of God and took Christ at His word. We were ready to be clay in the divine potter's hands and eager to be molded into the divine image. But the day has worn on and now noon has come and with it the midday sickness. It has crept upon us by stealth. We have faithfully attended worship, sung hymns, and listened to sermons but we are unaware that the youthful element of wonder has gone. We have God all figured out and we are no longer responsive to the whisper of the Spirit. Our hand is clasped over the egg cup and we say to ourselves "Now we've got Him!" Secure in the fixed rigid world that we have created in our minds it is easy to refuse to recognize that God is moving powerfully in new ways. We jealously guard our old habits and traditions and feel a vague sense of threat when our young people discover exciting new avenues of worship.

Of course it is right to stand firm on what is the essence of the faith once delivered to the saints. But we must beware lest under the disguise of conviction we hide the symptom of inflexibility that is a mark of the destruction

that wastes at noonday—the midday sickness. As Brian
Wren reminds us:

> *This is a day of new beginnings,*
> *Time to remember and move on.*

THE THIRD SYMPTOM— INORDINATE CRAVING FOR HUMAN APPROVAL

In considering human approval I am not, of course,
talking about affirmation. We all need to be encouraged and
affirmed. Some of us are quite miserly in our words of
appreciation. Heaven alone knows how much such affirmation would mean to many preachers, teachers,
musicians, youth workers, and parents. Every area of life
would be blessed by the refreshing rain of encouragement.
But there is a very significant difference between needing
a word of uplift and a life determined by a craving for
human approval.

Some years ago I attended a symphony concert given by
the famous Hallé Orchestra. I arrived with my family for
the performance and we studied the program. The first half
was to consist of works by Beethoven and Mozart and this
would be followed by an intermission of twenty minutes.
The second part of the concert was devoted to the first
performance of a modern composer's Fifth Symphony.

The program notes dismissed the first half of the
concert in about four terse lines. It gave a whole page,
however, to a detailed description of the new work to be
presented after the interval. It told us that in the first
movement we would be introduced to a musical phrase of
one of the great eighteenth century masters. Then in the
second and third movements we would hear this musical

phrase assailed on every side and that it would finally emerge triumphant and stand secure, the symphony concluding on a note of jubilation.

We enjoyed Beethoven and Mozart in the first half. During the interval we went out to enjoy our ice cream and lemonade. At the end of the interval the bell summoned us back for the second half. Nothing had prepared us for what followed. I suppose it is a commentary on my musical ignorance that I felt lost in a sea of meaningless noise. The conductor waved his baton with vehemence and the orchestra played with enthusiasm. I supposed they knew what they were doing. It meant little to me. I think I heard the musical phrase to which the program referred, but I could not be sure. I agreed with the program that this phrase was assailed on every side. Finally, the symphony finished with a triumphant discordant burst. It was for me a merciful relief. But what followed was stunning. The crowded hall erupted into the most enthusiastic applause. I was dumbfounded. Why on earth were they cheering? Then the composer was brought onto the platform and the applause became rapturous.

Judging from the response of the audience that night, the work I had just heard was destined for a place among the immortals. Yet here's the interesting thing. Although in the twenty-five years that have elapsed since that concert I have heard the works of Beethoven and Mozart scores of times, I have not *once* heard a performance of that fifth symphony. How unwise I would have been to have been guided by the enthusiasm of the crowd that night. Human applause can be seductive, fickle, and quite misleading.

A symptom of the midday sickness is an inordinate craving for this human applause. In our journey of faith our eye needs to be fixed not on human approval but the smile of heaven. When Peter and John were warned by the Jewish authorities of the dire consequences if they continued with their ministry, they answered in apostolic words: "Whether it is right in God's sight to listen to you rather than to God, you must judge; for we cannot keep from speaking about what we have seen and heard" (Acts 4:19). The only applause that really counted for them was the applause of Christ.

My friend Dr. A. S. Wood, once told me a story about Verdi that I have never forgotten. When Verdi was a young man he produced an opera written in a hurry. It was far below the standard of which he was capable. It was staged in Florence where the enthusiastic yet undiscriminating audience went into quite unwarranted raptures and cheered the composer to the echo. Had it been in Milan or Rome, the reception would have been very different. It is said that Verdi paid little heed to the cheers of the crowd. He raised his eyes to the box where sat the one whose approval he sought more than all else. The man in the box was altogether unimpressed, and he greeted the curtain calls at the end in stony silence. The man was the genius Rossini. Without his smile, the plaudits of the crowd meant nothing.

Through his hymns, Charles Wesley has left an imperishable legacy to the Methodist Church. How did the great poet of Methodism escape the midday sickness? We find the answer in the last lines that came from his lips and which his devoted wife wrote down. As his life ebbed away he whispered:

In age and feebleness extreme
Who can a worthless worm redeem?
Jesus! My only hope Thou art,
Source of my failing flesh and heart;

O could I catch one smile from Thee,
And drop into eternity!

The only applause he craved was that of his Savior.

The midday sickness is all around us. It can be seen in the gale of hurry which sweeps us up. It can be seen in the inflexibility that creeps over our souls. It can be seen in our craving for human approval. What of its cure?

Turn your eyes upon Jesus,
Look full in His wonderful face,
And the things of earth will grow strangely dim
In the light of His glory and grace.

When some stubbornly refused to believe
and spoke evil of the Way before the congregation,
he (Paul) left them, taking the disciples with him,
and argued daily in the lecture hall of Tyrannus.
This continued for two years,
so that all the residents of Asia, both Jews and Greeks
heard the word of the Lord.

ACTS 19:9–10 (NRSV)

Chapter Four

Conflict in a Classroom

June 1995

*I*t was a wedding to remember!

Like most ministers, I have had some unusual experiences in connection with weddings, but one in particular crowned them all. It happened early in my ministry when I was at the Central Hall, Westminster, and also serving the Methodist church in Chelsea, London.

The bride-to-be, Felicity, was the daughter of a Catholic father and an Anglican (Episcopalian) mother. The bride-groom was Italian. Felicity had been educated in an English convent school. After graduating from business college, she obtained a position in Rome. With her parentage and education, living so close to the Vatican and surrounded by thousands of eligible Catholic bachelors, it seemed inevitable that she would marry into the Church of Rome. Instead, she confounded all the odds and fell in love with an Italian Methodist! The wedding was duly planned for three o'clock at Chelsea Methodist church on a Saturday afternoon in May.

From an architectural point of view, the church was unpromising. At that time, the sanctuary had not been rebuilt after being destroyed by bombs during the war. Worship and other activities continued in a large fellowship hall that stood above a row of shops on the most fashionable road in Chelsea.

Knowing the bride's background I realized that leaders in society would be attending the ceremony. I was determined to make sure that what we could not offer in architectural beauty, we would make up for in skillful organization.

The bride wanted a normal, simple English ceremony. This meant that the guests would arrive to the sound of suitable organ music. We were blessed with a talented organist. He arrived early and took his place at the keyboard with his back to the congregation. He glanced regularly through a rearview mirror so that he would see when the bridal party had arrived and was in position. Then he would strike up the "Wedding March" and the bride would process down the aisle with her father followed by the bridesmaids. It was all perfectly straightforward. What could possibly go wrong?

Just before the appointed hour, the limousine carrying Felicity and her father to the church sputtered to an unscheduled stop in Sloane Square, Chelsea. We were never told what the problem was, but it took the harassed driver twenty minutes to put it right. Meanwhile, at the church we passed the three o'clock deadline. The bride's mother and the groom's parents were looking at their watches. Our custodian was getting anxious. I was already very worried. The best man was terrified and the bridegroom was about to faint away. The organist, who had been playing since 2:30 P.M., reached the end of his prepared repertoire. With great presence of mind, he turned the music over and started from the beginning once more. As he played, he kept looking into the mirror waiting for a sign from the custodian that the bride had arrived.

At long last the signal was given. With a sigh of relief, the organist launched into Wagner's "Wedding March." As the congregation stood, I positioned myself at the altar rail in the usual way, beckoning the bridegroom and best man to join me there. The bride and her father, however, did not appear. The organist played on and the rest of us stood in bewildered suspense. We had not bargained for the intervention of society magazine photographers. They besieged the bride at the church door with their flashing cameras while we in the church stood and waited. The organist reached the end of the "Wedding March" and began it a second time, keeping his eye on the mirror for the appearance of the bridal party. When Felicity eventually entered, worried at having kept everyone waiting, she hurried her father down the aisle to join the bridegroom at the altar rail. Unfortunately, at the critical moment, the organist took his eyes off the mirror and missed her entry. Since the altar rail was not in his line of vision, he was unaware that she had arrived. He played on and we all stood waiting. Finally, there was no alternative but to bellow above the sound of the organ, "Dearly beloved, we are gathered together here in the sight of God. . . . " The organ music faded away, and the service began.

There followed what seemed a catalog of things going wrong because we were all in a state of nervous agitation. All my careful plans to impress our visitors were frustrated. Yet quite remarkably, of all the many weddings I have conducted over the years, this one yielded the most positive results. Many guests in the congregation returned to worship with us. The bride and groom were ecstatic. Their parents were thrilled. Everyone was absolutely delighted. Looking back, I could see that God was in that situation reminding me that His ways are not always our ways, and that He is able to use our foolishness to praise Him.

I thought about that experience when I read in Acts 19 that Paul used the lecture hall of Tyrannus in Ephesus for two years as his church. Because Luke's account is tantalizingly brief, it is easy to overlook the fact that the apostle spent longer in Ephesus than anywhere else. His ministry there lasted for nearly three years (Acts 20:31). I wish Luke had told us more. We do know, however, that Paul used the lecture hall of Tyrannus the philosopher. There in that classroom a titanic conflict took place between the spirit of God and the spirit of the age. It is a conflict which each succeeding generation of believers has to face. There, in that classroom, four of the claims which are made by the spirit of the age were exposed as false.

The Spirit of the Age Says the Place is Wrong

It is generally supposed that a successful church needs a warm, attractive building to encourage people to attend worship. Such a building makes work amongst the young easier. It has a greater appeal for a young bride. It makes the congregation feel comfortable coming, as many do, from pleasant, bright, warm homes. Surely this is entirely proper because only the best is good enough for God.

How can God be expected to work in such an unlikely place as a classroom? The lecture hall of Tyrannus is not conducive for worship, and it is certainly not an appropriate setting for preaching. It seems to be simply the wrong place in which to start a church.

Throughout my medical career, when opportunity has presented itself without being intrusive, I have encouraged both colleagues and patients to talk about their faith. During my first year in family medicine, I noticed that time and again the ministry of one particular church in the area featured in such conversations. My interest was aroused, and one Sunday evening I went there to worship. My first impression was not favorable. The building was an example of gloomy Victorian architecture. The welcome at the door was gracious and warm, but the entrance was dimly lit. I chose the balcony to get a better view, and noticed the stairs were bare boards. My conclusion was that the building needed a complete renovation.

The church was packed! There was a buzz of excitement. It was not a Methodist church, so the form of service was new to me, but the worship was powerful. The preacher, a little Welshman, was unimpressive in appearance. He began his sermon in a quiet, deliberate tone—almost like a teacher addressing a class of students. Then, after the manner of some of the great Welsh preachers, his voice mounted in intensity and grew in passion as he became absorbed in his theme. He seemed to catch fire! We in the congregation were caught up by his message. I lost sight of the messenger. I lost sight of the dingy building and its dim lighting. I was in another place with angels and archangels and all the company of heaven. It was magnificent, exhilarating, uplifting, and powerfully moving.

I walked home from that service marvelling at the power of God and feeling chastened. I had almost allowed the *spirit of the age* to influence my thinking as it cried, "Not here!" From a human perspective, the place *was* inadequate. God, however, thought otherwise. My experience that night was a powerful reminder that when the Holy Spirit is present, any place becomes God-appointed.

The spirit of the age would say that John Wesley ought to have had his life-changing experience in St. Paul's Cathedral when he was there on May 24, 1738. The awesome masterpiece by Sir Christopher Wren was surely an appropriate setting for such a historic spiritual encounter. The Holy Spirit thought otherwise. That very evening in a simple room on Aldersgate Street, a work of grace occurred which caused the restless Anglican clergyman to feel his heart strangely warmed. In such an unlikely place, a fire began to burn in Wesley's life that set England and the world aglow.

The spirit of the age would judge Bethlehem, an insignificant backwater town in the Roman world, to be entirely inappropriate for the birth of the Savior. As for being born in a stable, that would be nothing less than an outrage. The proper birthplace for a king would be Rome in the palace of the Emperor. The spirit of God thought otherwise.

The spirit of the age would say that Nazareth was the wrong place from which to launch a teaching ministry. Athens would be the proper starting place for a teacher. *The spirit of the age* would say that Calvary was the wrong place to save a lost humanity. A throne would be the appropriate place for a redeemer, not a cross.

The world sees the lecture hall of Tyrannus and cries, "This is the wrong place." It is a lie! God's ways are not our ways, and God says, "It is not the place, it is the heart that matters." When men and women respond to Christ in penitence and faith, regardless of the place, a glorious work of grace begins.

THE SPIRIT OF THE AGE SAYS THE TIME IS WRONG

A few miles from my home was a small country chapel where I often preached before I entered the ministry. It was the unusual custom in that community for the men to come together for worship in the afternoon and then to return with their families in the evening for a second service.

Sunday afternoon services have never been my favorites! One cold November Sunday afternoon we gathered in the small sanctuary. As usual, the men, who worked out-of-doors all week in agriculture, had enjoyed a large hot lunch. In the chapel, a huge potbellied stove had brought the temperature to a dangerously comfortable level. The windows were tightly shut. The conditions were perfect for slumber. No preacher stood a chance! Before I had even announced my text, some of my congregation were already nodding. I did everything I could to keep them awake. I pounded the pulpit. I stomped on the floor. I raised my voice and clapped my hands, all to no avail. First one and then another dropped off until almost all of them were soundly asleep. One or two valiant souls fought against the inclination with glazed eyes. Had they joined the majority, I could have pronounced the blessing and brought the service to a close.

There is an interesting footnote in the New Revised Standard Version of Acts 19:9. It derives from reliable manuscripts. These record that Paul occupied the lecture hall of Tyrannus from eleven in the morning until four in the afternoon ("from the fifth to the tenth hour"). Why was that small detail mentioned?

Imagine the heat of Ephesus! It is obvious why Tyrannus did not use his lecture hall at that time of the day. This skillful sophist philosopher lectured in the cool of the morning to the wide-eyed, fresh young noblemen who could spare the time to indulge their intellectual appetites. He resumed his lecturing in the late afternoon when the sun was setting. Between the hours of eleven and four, like all other sensible people in Ephesus, he rested. Tyrannus was not foolish enough to struggle for his hearers' attention when they were thinking about a siesta.

This was the very time Paul took over the lecture hall. It was available because it was an inconvenient hour. Here in this classroom we are reminded of one of the areas of conflict between the spirit of God and the spirit of the age. Paul, God's advocate, was not out to win men and women by appealing to what was convenient. He recognized that there was a price involved in following Christ. The spirit of the world cries out, "Put convenience first. Find a convenient time." The spirit of God says, "Put Christ first and use the time you have."

When we set out to serve God, we may be sure that the spirit of the age will try to dissuade us with the cry, "This is the wrong time"—and it is a lie! Here in this conflict in the classroom we are reminded that every moment can become God's appointed time.

THE SPIRIT OF THE AGE SAYS THIS IS THE WRONG CONGREGATION

The rules for any movement to have an impact on the community are well known. Chief among these is that it must be supported by those who have an esteemed place in society and who wield influence. Such people give a church standing.

Tyrannus knew the rules. This sophist philosopher would have collected around him young, aristocratic, intelligent men. He would not want the elderly; after all, great movements need the young. He would not welcome people of lowly birth; his target group would be the upper class who had influence. He would not want those of modest intellect; he would be aiming at the intelligentsia. In common with all teachers of philosophy, he would have restricted his school to men.

Paul scorned these rules. He collected around him all the wrong sort of people. His congregation included slaves, the uneducated, the poor, the outcasts, and most significantly, women. "There are few of us who are noble or mighty," he wrote to the Corinthians. "God has chosen the weak things of this world to confound the strong and the foolish things of this world to confound the wise" (1 Cor. 1:27–28). Paul recognized dignity and nobility in ordinary folk. He saw each of them as having exquisite worth because of what they meant to God.

The Edinburgh Festival is an annual gathering place for all who are interested in the visual and performing arts, and each year it attracts great crowds to Scotland. An incident took place in the early years of the festival which has often been retold. A middle-aged man approached the desk in the crowded lobby of a hotel in the city and asked for a room. The clerk behind the desk addressed him in a voice that could be heard by every person in the lobby. "A room?" he said in a note of sarcastic incredulity. "Are you seriously asking for a room? Don't you know that we are in the midst of the Edinburgh Festival? We have been fully booked for weeks." The man shrugged his shoulders, thanked the clerk, and turned away. As he left the desk, he was surrounded by journalists who begged him for an interview. The clerk looked at the scene in bewilderment. Turning to a man standing by, he asked, "What is all that about? Who is he?" The man looked at the clerk in astonishment. "Why!" he exclaimed, "Don't you know? Did you not recognize him? That is Pablo Casals, the greatest cellist in the world." The clerk realized he had blundered. "Mr. Casals," he called out, "of course we can find *you* a room. I did not realize you were somebody special."

What makes a person special? Tyrannus, representing the spirit of the age, says that depends upon nobility of birth, social position, intellectual attainment, or wealth—and it is a lie! Paul, representing the spirit of Christ, reaches out to the least, the last, and the lowest. Charles Wesley expresses Paul's response to the selectivity of Tyrannus and the spirit of the age with his uncompromising lines:

The world He suffered to redeem;
For all He hath the atonement made;.

For those that will not come to Him
The ransom of His life was paid.

THE SPIRIT OF THE AGE SAYS THE MESSAGE IS WRONG

In June 1993 when preaching in St. Ives, Cornwall, I visited a historic Methodist church. I was particularly impressed by a door that led from the sanctuary into a large fellowship hall. This door is known as the "Cook door." The walls around it are nearly two-feet thick. Beside it is a framed marker that explains how it received its name. My guide, the local minister, filled in the background.

An evangelist named Thomas Cook, renowned for his Christlike holiness, visited that church in 1890. His visit was preceded by controversy. Some said he was old-fashioned in his approach and did not have the right message for that day and that church. "What we need," some of them said, "is a preacher who is better educated and more in tune with the spirit of our age." These gloomy prophets predicted that people would not respond to Cook's message and the mission would fail.

Thomas Cook arrived on a Saturday afternoon to begin a ten-day evangelistic mission. Before he unpacked, he asked his host to take him to the church. It is a large sanctuary with a center pulpit and a balcony on three sides. Cook asked what provision had been made for an enquiry room where he could counsel those who came seeking Christ. He was shown a small room behind the pulpit. The evangelist looked at the room and then diffidently shook his head. "I am afraid this will not be big enough," he said. He returned to the sanctuary and stood facing the pulpit. He pointed to his left. "What is behind that wall?" he asked. "Why, the fellowship hall," his host replied. "To enter it you have to go out the back door of the church into the street. You then reenter the hall by a separate door." As soon as he saw the fellowship hall, Thomas Cook knew it was exactly what was required. "This must be my enquiry room," he said. "Is it possible to make a doorway between the sanctuary and that hall?"

During the hours of Saturday night and Sunday morning, members of the church broke through the two-feet thick walls and made a door. This is commemorated by the plaque that concludes, "In the following ten days, seven hundred men and women passed through this door seeking Christ as their Savior."

In that old Methodist church in St. Ives, Cornwall, the conflict of the classroom took place. There were some in that church who would have preferred the words of Tyrannus, but what was needed was the message of Paul. Advocates for Tyrannus are everywhere. They speak for the spirit of the age and reject moral absolutes. They do not accept that certain things are everlastingly right and others everlastingly wrong. These modern sophists believe prudence is the guiding light in all matters of behavior. So long as what we do has no obvious harmful consequences and provided adequate precautions are taken, why have a scruple? Sin, so far as they are concerned, is a misfortune when an action misfires—but no great matter. Better luck next time.

The message which Paul brought to that lecture hall and brings to us today is in complete contrast. He does not come teaching about prudence but about sin and forgiveness. He tells us of a crucified Savior who takes our stained and shattered lives and by a glorious act of grace cleanses and restores. He offers a message of hope in a world of hopelessness, not just for sunny days in calm weather, but also for dark nights in the storm. Paul tells of One who comes to us when we are overwhelmed by grief, distress, shame, and guilt and brings a new beginning. This Jesus of whom he speaks knows our hearts and our deepest needs.

In my youth I heard a preacher tell us about a brave man who died in the service of his country. He left behind a sick widow and an eight-year-old son. The hero was posthumously awarded the highest honor for valor that his grateful nation could bestow, the Victoria Cross. The widow and her son were invited to Buckingham Palace for the investiture. It was a small private ceremony at which several outstanding men and women were to be honored. As the mother and her son took their place amongst the gathering, she was overcome with a great sense of fear. Because of her illness, she found it difficult to stand. What if her legs gave way and she fell when the king came in? Just then an official came into the chamber and went round quietly speaking to each person explaining what had to be done when the all-important moment arrived. He came to the widow and put her at her ease. Before he left he said casually, "Oh, and by the way, when the king comes in and everyone stands, you are to remain seated. Don't bother to get up. *The king knows.*"

The King knows about me! He knows about my hopes and my failures. He knows how I struggle against temptation and yet fall. He knows how I long to be a better person. He knows about the things that worry me. He knows about my pain and sorrow. Tyrannus cannot say that. It is a message only the gospel can proclaim.

We are in the lecture hall of Tyrannus. We are in the midst of the conflict in the classroom. A titanic battle is taking place in our day between the spirit of God and the spirit of the age. Tyrannus, the spirit of the age, is after the ear of our generation. God is after its *heart*. We have a choice to make. Are we going to listen to the call of the world through its advocate, Tyrannus, or are we going to listen to the call of Christ through the apostle Paul?

What shall I return to the Lord
for all his bounty to me?
I will lift up the cup of salvation
and call on the name of the Lord.

PSALM 116:12–13 (NRSV)

Giving thanks to God the Father
at all times and for everything
in the name of our Lord Jesus Christ.

EPHESIANS 5:20 (NRSV)

Chapter Five

The Grace of Gratitude

July 1997

O ne of my friends in theological seminary was a visiting scholar from Germany. He was in his second year there when I arrived and was one of the first persons to welcome me. I later learned that he had come loaded with academic distinctions. He was an intellectual greyhound, light years ahead of the rest of us in biblical studies. As we struggled with the basics of Hebrew and Greek to satisfy the examiners at London University, he was happily researching obscure subjects in Aramaic for a book he was writing. He had a delightful sense of humor and enjoyed our laughter when he stumbled over some unusual English expression. We, his friends, found it comforting to know that such a brilliant scholar who was at home in all the languages of antiquity could have problems with the English idiom. It meant he was human after all.

One evening when we were chatting over coffee, he told us of an experience he had the previous year. "I had only been in England about six weeks," he said. "Everyone teased me because whenever I said 'thank you' I always added 'very much.' Evidently I said those two extra words with great emphasis, and it sometimes sounded strange. For example, if I were given change in a store, a ticket on a bus, or handed a hymnal in the chapel I would always say, 'thank you very much.' Then one of the students here told me that for a minor kindness it was not necessary to say more than a simple 'thank you.' He said that in England you tended to reserve the extra words 'very much' for more special occasions otherwise it sounded a bit 'over the top.' I took the advice literally," he said. Then he smiled ruefully and went on to tell us the rest of the story.

Two weeks after receiving this advice he was invited to preach at a small church just outside London. An elderly lady in the congregation approached him after the service. "I live just opposite the train station," she said. "Your train to London is not due for over an hour. Would you like to come and have a cup of coffee at my house while you are waiting?" He then told us how he gratefully accepted this gracious offer. When the time came for him to take his leave, he wanted to express appreciation but was anxious for it not to sound exaggerated. He hesitated, then remembered what he had been told. "Thank you," he said and added with a smile, "but not very much."

He was invited to return to that church several times during his stay in London. On each occasion he was reminded of this incident which the lady concerned and her friends delighted to relate. It was remembered long after his sermons had been forgotten.

The Bible takes gratitude very seriously. Jesus takes five barley loaves, "and when he had given thanks" (John 6:11) feeds a multitude. At the grave of Lazarus before calling his dead friend back to life he says "Father, I thank you for having heard me" (John 11:42). In the night in which He was betrayed he took a cup of wine and a loaf and gave thanks. Paul calls upon believers, "In everything by prayer and supplication with thanksgiving let your requests be made known to God" (Phil. 4:6). Repeatedly in his writings the note of thanksgiving rings out. "Joyfully giving thanks to the Father who has enabled us to share in the inheritance of the saints in light" (Col. 1:2). "Thanks be to God for His incredible gift" (2 Cor. 9:15).

But how do we express our gratitude to God? This is the question the psalmist addresses and then goes on to provide the answer. "What shall I return to the Lord for all his bounty to me? I will lift up the cup of salvation and call on the name of the Lord." Here in the grace of gratitude it is possible to trace three fundamental steps in Christian growth.

THE FIRST STEP—RECOGNIZING OUR DEBT

For many years the great annual event in the British Scout movement was a spectacular theatrical production staged in London. The *Gang Show* as it was called, played to capacity audiences for two weeks. It was a magical combination of singing, dramatic sketches, humour, pathos, and much exuberance. The presiding genius was the gifted London stage producer Ralph Raeder for whom it was a labor of love. He drew on the vast source of talent in the tens of thousands of scouts all over the country. The songs from the *Gang Show* became part of Boy Scout lore and were sung at campfires around the world.

One year I was fortunate enough to obtain one of the much prized tickets and attended a performance. What an experience that was! Come with me and glimpse over my shoulder at one of the items.

As the curtain rises we see before us a Victorian winter scene. It is Christmas day and we are gazing from our seats in the balcony on a church gate with a path winding away from us to the sanctuary doors. Standing by the gate are two men in conversation. We quickly learn that one of them is the author Charles Dickens.

As the two men talk someone approaches. We recognize him immediately. His jaunty, swaggering gait, his florid complexion, his top hat tilted at a rakish angle, and his ornate walking stick mark him out. There can be only one man like that. This must be Wilkins Macawber, immortalized in the novel *David Copperfield*. Dickens doffs his hat and greets him. "A merry Christmas to you, Mr. Macawber." Macawber looks at the author in surprise. He holds up his silver knobbed walking stick in acknowledgement and with a flourish replies "I thank you, Sir. And a merry Christmas to you, whoever you might be." With no further word of greeting he walks past the two men along the path to the church.

A moment or two later a couple approaches; David Copperfield and Agnes. "A Merry Christmas to you Mr. and Mrs. Copperfield," Dickens says. David raises his hat and replies, "And also to you, Sir, although I don't believe we have had the pleasure of making your acquaintance." Then he and his wife pass by into the church.

Along comes an older man. He has happiness written all over him. We can tell at once that it is the converted Ebenezer Scrooge. "A Merry Christmas to you Mr. Scrooge," the author says. Scrooge looks pleasantly surprised and warmly replies, "And also to you. How kind of you to greet a stranger thus." And he passes by into the church. There follow many of the characters from the various novels of Charles Dickens on their way to the church. Each of them is greeted by the author and each responds as though speaking to a stranger.

When they have all filed past and entered the church for the Christmas morning service the two men are left standing alone at the gate. Before going up the path themselves and joining the congregation they gaze in silence at the building. We hear the strains of the opening carol which the congregation is singing: "Hark the herald angels sing." At this point the companion of Charles Dickens, who has remained silent during the exchange of greetings, turns to the distinguished author and says in a bewildered tone, "How very strange that none of those people who spoke to you recognized their creator." And then the curtain comes down.

We are left to reflect upon his words. We are lost in our busy world, chasing after things and ignoring God. "How strange that so few recognize their Creator."

But why should they? Why is it so important to recognize our indebtedness to God? Does he want to be thanked for creating us? Were we not taught as children that good deeds are to be performed for their own sake and not for appreciation? Why then is the Bible always exhorting us to be thankful? To grapple, even superficially, with this vast subject takes us into deep water.

Luke tells us that Jesus healed ten men suffering from leprosy. We need no reminding of how loathsome a disease this was. It brought with it not only physical disfigurement but also a social sentence. That sentence was isolation. The poor sufferers were forbidden to visit their homes, their families, their villages, or their places of worship. For them, there were no family joys of a new baby, a wedding, or any anniversary. They could not even share in the somber comforts of a family funeral. Banished from the community, they endured a living death as beggars. In Luke's story, Jesus takes pity on the ten and tells them to go and show themselves to the priests. The priests were the public health officials of the day and only they could remove the social stigma, lift the sentence and give these unfortunate wretches

official permission to return to their homes. As the ten set off
they realize that their disease has gone. Imagine it! Suddenly
a crippling burden has been lifted from their shoulders. Yet
only one returns to express gratitude. Luke adds that he was
a despised Samaritan. Jesus appears surprised. "Were there
not ten healed?" he asks. "Then where are the other nine?"
Then he says to the Samaritan, "Go on your way; your faith
has made you whole." But were not the other nine also cured?
What did Jesus mean when he said to this tenth man, "Your
faith has made you whole"? What has this one received that
was denied the others? The answer lies in recognizing two
kinds of disease. There is a leprosy of the body from which all
ten were healed. There is also a leprosy which comes from a
spirit incapable of gratitude. This Samaritan had been
cleansed of both and is, therefore, truly whole. In other
words, gratitude is important not for God's sake but for ours.

There is a well-known story attributed to Winston
Churchill of a sailor who dived into Plymouth Sound to
rescue a boy who had fallen into the deep water. Modestly
the rescuer slipped away before any fuss could be made
over his gallant action. Later that day when the boy was
in the High Street with his mother he spotted the sailor.
He nudged her and whispered, "That's the man who saved
my life." Immediately the woman rushed across to the
sailor. "Are you the man who dived into the water this
morning and brought out my boy?" she asked. "Yes,
madam" said the sailor. "Then," said the woman with
mounting anger, "Where's his cap?" The sad thing was not
what her ingratitude did to the sailor but what it did to
her. She was diminished by it.

When we pause to admire the beauty of a painting by
Peter Breughel, Cannoletto, or Rubens, we are not doing
something for them. They are beyond our praise. We do

something for ourselves. The appreciation enlarges and
ennobles our spirit. When we listen approvingly to the music
of Brahms, Chopin, or Mozart we are not ̶doing anything for
them, we are enriching ourselves. As we respond to beauty
our lives are enhanced. So it is when we respond to God in
gratitude. Through it we ourselves are ennobled and we
grow in grace.

It is not for God's sake but for ours that a grateful heart
is essential.

THE SECOND STEP—LONGING TO REPAY THE DEBT

Ignoring good advice, I once lent a small sum of money to
a certain individual. I was serving my two years of National
Service at the time. My comrades had warned me not to be
taken in by this particular man. He had acquired an
unsavory reputation through borrowing and never repaying.
I was told that each newcomer had been beguiled by his
pleading stories.

Sure enough, about two weeks after my arrival he paid
me a visit. I was in my room studying. He entered to find me
surrounded by my Bible and several commentaries on loan
from the Unit Library. The time to ask a Christian a favor is
when he has his Bible in his hand! I was treated to a
heartrending story. It was a work of art. He wanted to send
a gift home to his mother. Because he wanted it to arrive on
her birthday, he could not wait until pay day. He promised
me faithfully with deep earnestness that the first thing he
would do when he received his pay would be to return what
he had borrowed. My initial skepticism founded on the
warnings of my friends was swept away by his sincere
entreaties. I gave him the loan and hoped that my trust
would be rewarded.

In the weeks that followed it was perfectly obvious that he recognized his debt. He studiously avoided me! If he saw me approaching from one direction he would suddenly have an urgent errand that sent him the opposite way. He recognized his debt all right but he had no intention of repaying it. In fact he never did!

Contrast him with another man who was so very different.

In my final year in seminary I was asked to preach at a church on the outskirts of London. The resident minister had suddenly been taken ill and a substitute was needed for both the Sunday morning and evening services. After the morning service I was told that I was to be entertained by a very distinguished member of the congregation. I learned that he had retired early from the diplomatic service and loved to provide hospitality for visiting preachers. I found him waiting for me outside the church. He was tall, about sixty years of age, with silver grey hair, and a naturally dignified bearing. He smiled and shook my hand warmly. Then he opened the rear door of his handsome car and I got in. I noticed a lady sitting in the front passenger seat. She was slumped over, evidently unable to sit upright. My host introduced her. She was his wife. When we arrived at the beautiful Tudor house where they lived my host went to the trunk of the car and brought out a folding wheelchair. Very gently, he lifted his wife into it and wheeled her up the narrow pathway to the large oak front door. I followed. There were roses everywhere. The whole of the front of the house was covered in roses and the path was arched with them.

Lunch was a cold buffet and had been prepared before they had set out for church. Tenderly he lifted the frail form of his wife to the table. He sat beside her and cut up her food. Then he fed her. Throughout the meal he proved to be a fascinating conversationalist. I noticed how carefully he included his wife interpreting her almost inaudible whispers without the slightest embarrassment or hesitation. After the meal he lifted her from her chair at the table to a couch. How tender and careful he was with her! He then took a blanket and covered her with it because, even though it was June, it was cool in that Tudor house. He and I did the washing up; he washed and I dried. It was before the days of dishwashers.

Afterwards he invited me to walk with him around his lovely garden and yard at the back of the house. We came to a little arbor where there was a seat. We sat amongst roses; they arched over us. To this day whenever I smell the fragrance of the rose, I think of that house and that moment. I felt rather awkward in the presence of such a distinguished person, the recipient of so many honors. There was a pause in our conversation. Breaking the silence I said, "I think it is wonderful what you are doing for your wife." He smiled and patted my knee affectionately and said, "My dear boy, let me tell you about that remarkable woman. She has done everything for me. I could have accomplished nothing without her. When I set out in the diplomatic service she subordinated all her own personal ambitions and desires to further my career. We had four boys. She brought them up almost single-handed. I was all too often an absentee father because of my work. And then the war came. Did you ever read how in 1941 the battle cruiser *Hood* was blown up by a chance shell from the German battleship *Bismarck* with the loss of fifteen hundred men?" I nodded. It was a well known story. "Our oldest son was on that ship." He said. "I fell apart when I learned of his death but that wonderful woman, in spite of her own grief, held me together. Then our second son died at the battle of El Alemein and again I fell apart. Once again she held me together. Always she was doing things for me. Even when she was struck by multiple sclerosis she carried on without a complaint until she was finally unable to stand or walk. And I want to tell you this." He paused. He was struggling to hold back tears. He swallowed hard and then whispered with great emphasis, "As long as there is breath in my body I want to try to repay a little of what she has done for me."

There is something very noble in a spirit like that. He had moved from the first to the second stage in the grace of gratitude. He not only recognized his debt, he longed to pay it back. Lift that into the spiritual realm. The psalmist challenges us to fill our lives with a longing to repay God for all His goodness towards us; "What shall I return to the Lord for all his bounty to me?" John Wesley experienced it. He translated some lines of the great German hymn writer Paulus Gerhardt that express it eloquently:

> *My Savior! how shall I proclaim,*
> *How pay the mighty debt I owe?*
> *Let all I have, and all I am,*
> *Ceaseless to all Thy glory show.*

THE THIRD STEP—DISCOVERING HOW TO REPAY

If we have made the first two steps in the grace of gratitude—the recognition of our debt and then the longing to repay—we have come far. But we have yet to take the most important step on our journey. After all, how can we pay God back? Everything we have is His already. Paul even goes beyond that and tells us that even what is best in us, that which he refers to as "righteousness" is like "a dirty rag" when seen against God's sublime purity and awesome goodness.

I remember wondering how I could ever repay my parents for what they had done for me. I realized I owed them everything. Although they could not afford it, they had ensured I had the best possible education. How I longed to do something in return! When I left college and enlisted for my required military service I signed a form that meant a portion of my pay would be deducted each week and sent home to my parents. It was not much but at least it was something. I found comfort in thinking after my discharge that over the two years I had made at least a token repayment.

That remained my illusion until the day I set off for theological seminary. My father accompanied me to the train. He was a man of little conversation and we each carried a suitcase in silence. I boarded the train, put the suitcases on the racks, and lowered the window. We exchanged pleasantries until the guard blew the whistle and waived his flag. It was then that my father reached into his inside pocket and brought out an envelope. "Here," he said, "This is yours. Look after yourself and don't forget to write." With that he turned and walked off the platform. He didn't look back, that was not his style.

I sat in the train compartment as it left the station, my mind in a daze of excitement. My thoughts were on what lay ahead of me. So many had assured me that seminary days would be very special and my expectations caused my heart to race. About twenty minutes passed before I thought about the envelope my father had put into my hand. I opened it and took out a small green book. It was a bank savings book in my name. Puzzled, I turned the pages. What I saw was profoundly moving. There was a long list of entries. Every penny I had ever sent home was entered there together with an equal amount that my parents had deposited out of their slender resources. I had imagined I was paying them back. Instead I was slipping deeper and deeper into debt.

This is how it is with God. There is no way in which anyone can repay the debt. The more we do for Him the more enriched we are. God out-gives us every time. How then can we repay the debt? With the psalmist we cry, "What shall I return to the Lord for all his bounty towards me?" It is the psalmist himself who provides the answer. He points to the secret of the third step in the grace of gratitude. He goes on to say "I will lift up the cup of salvation and call upon the name of the Lord." Here is the glorious paradox of the Christian faith. We pay God back by taking more! We repay by accepting the salvation that has been provided in Christ. In one of his great hymns Charles Wesley expresses this truth turning these words of the Psalmist into Christian verse:

> *What shall I render to my God*
> *For all His mercies store?*
> *I'll take the gifts He hath bestowed*
> *And humbly ask for more.*

But isn't this too facile? Does this not make for too easy a creed? If we think it too easy then we have lost sight of the tremendous life-changing power of gratitude. When we get the goodness of God fixed in our heart, when we turn to Christ and accept his offered cup of salvation, our lives become possessed by a burning desire to spend our days in devoted service. Consider the saints. Look at Wesley or Francis Xavier or Mother Theresa. What was it that drove them? A desire to earn favor? A desire to make a name? A desire to save their souls? No, never! It was rather an all consuming gratitude to God for what had been done for them in the work of salvation.

The third step in the grace of gratitude is the acceptance of the cup of salvation. This is God's delightful surprise. As we receive it we are filled with an overwhelming sense of thanksgiving. Gratitude so fills our hearts that we find a passionate longing to serve God with our whole being. This sense of gratitude causes us gladly and eagerly to take up the yoke of Christ. As we reach out to receive the gift of salvation our thankful hearts discover that through this grace of gratitude the yoke becomes easy and the burden strangely light.

"What shall I return to the Lord for all his bounty to me? I will lift up the cup of salvation and call upon the name of the Lord."

†

On a Sabbath Jesus was teaching in one of the synagogues,
and a woman was there
who had been crippled by a spirit for eighteen years.
She was bent over and could not straighten up at all.
When Jesus saw her, he called her forward and said to her,
"Woman, you are set free from your infirmity."
Then he put his hands on her,
and immediately she straightened up and praised God.

LUKE 13:10–13 (NIV)

Walk Tall

July 1988

uring the summer of 1940, I used to go to the indoor public swimming pool with my school friends on Saturday mornings.

The way back to the bus stop took us beside the fish market where we used to see a little man. You could hardly miss him because even on the hottest days he wore a long raincoat that reached down to his ankles and on his head he wore a rather ridiculous looking top hat. He used to push a baby carriage in which there was a gramophone. The carriage was covered in patriotic posters announcing what would happen to Hitler and his gang and telling us to keep our chins up despite the air raids and the bombing. He appeared to be a harmless chap who played cheerful morale boosting records. He relied for a living on passersby who would take pity on him and put coins in a box that hung at the front of the carriage.

Now we children thought that we knew the truth about this man. We believed that he was a spy planted in our fish market by the Nazi High Command to undermine the British war effort. We reasoned that he was hiding his espionage under a great show of false patriotism that all his posters and music proclaimed. He did not, however, fool us. We had penetrated his secret and we *knew* that the harmless looking gramophone was really a disguised radio transmitter and that he was passing on vital information concerning activity in our fish market that would be most helpful for an enemy victory. We therefore did not shrink from striking blows for liberty by giving the baby carriage a push each time we passed it and then running away.

Of course it was all nonsense. Foolish childish ideas. The man was no more a spy than was Winston Churchill. Our wild fancies about this poor man were just figments of our childish imaginations.

Looking back I think I know why that dear harmless man appeared so sinister to us children. *He was bent almost double.* To our silly childish minds he stooped because he was trying to hide his face, a sure sign of guilt. We never actually looked him in the eyes. Much later when I studied medicine, I learned about the terrible condition of Ankylosing Spondilitis and then realized what was wrong with that man. I would give much to be able to go to him now, bend down, look him in the eyes, and tell him how sorry I am that we misjudged him so. I think he would probably smile and tell me that he understood.

Here in the gospel story is a woman who has been bent double for *eighteen years*. Think of it! Eighteen years looking at the pavement. Eighteen years not able to look up at the sun and the stars! Eighteen years not able to look others in the eyes. It is significant that the incident is only recorded by Luke the physician. No doubt he included the story in his narrative in order to introduce the teaching of Jesus about the keeping of regulations governing the Sabbath. It is, however, worthy of closer attention for its own sake.

WHERE HEALING TOOK PLACE—THE SYNAGOGUE

Wallace Hamilton was a much loved Methodist preacher in the United States. He told of how the pastor of a downtown church was jolted out of a mediocre ministry by a sharp question asked by a casual visitor in his congregation.

The morning was hot and stuffy and the service lacked any inspiration. The congregation was small and sleepy. From behind their waving fans they looked not too hopefully toward the pulpit where the preacher, evidently ill-prepared, struggled with his sermon and didn't do well. It was an ineffective performance.

When it was over he stood at the church door as usual to greet his congregation as they filed out. "Hot day Reverend," one man said. "Yes, dreadful," he replied. "Good morning Brother Robin," said another, "I hope it rains today." "Yes," the preacher answered, "that would be a blessing." And so one by one, the congregation said some perfunctory word as each left the church. Then suddenly he was shaking hands with a stranger. And something in the eyes and bearing of the man made the preacher uneasy. "My name is Robin," said the preacher. "Yes, I know," the stranger answered. "And you?" inquired the minister. "Only a watchman," the stranger replied. "A watchman," the minister repeated. "Yes," the man said. "Well we're glad to have you in church," the minister said. "Come again sir, come again." And then came the question, a sharp stinging word, "*Why?*" The preacher didn't see any more people after that though he continued to shake hands. He no longer heard what they said as they filed out. One word drummed in his ears, "Why?" "Come again." "Why?"[1]

Is there something happening in church that will make us want to come again? I am uncomfortable with gimmicks and artificial attempts to be sensational. Worship is too awesome a business for that. But it is sad when worship is dull.

Something happened in the synagogue that day because Jesus was present. And where there is true worship He always is present and something momentous inevitably happens. Broken hearts are mended. Spiritually blind eyes see again. Hard spirits are melted. Enmities are ended. It is so easy to talk *down* the church, to criticize it, and to parade its shortcomings. We need to talk *up* the church and recall all the blessings we have received from it.

The church ought to be a therapeutic community, a place where the walking wounded come to find comfort and healing. The church ought to be a sign of the Kingdom, that the reign of God is already breaking in upon the earth. And we need to thank God for all those who come bringing their bent backs, their scarred lives, and their abject spirits and find renewal and life because Christ is there: *"His touch has still its ancient power."*

Look out across any congregation and there will be someone there who has spondylitis in one form or another. Perhaps it is one who has damaged emotions, a victim of abuse inflicted by those who ought to have offered love. Or perhaps the problem is unconfessed and unresolved sin with a crippling burden of hideous mental images from a guilty past. Or perhaps there is one who is stooped over because of disillusionment, feeling betrayed by those who were trusted. Or again, perhaps the affliction is disappointment with all the brokenness of shattered hopes and dreams.

Will worship be for these bent persons a liberating experience as it was for the woman in the synagogue? Will they want to come again because they have been touched and made whole? Will they leave the house of God walking tall?

The One to Whom the Healing Came—The Patient

It is easy to suppose that this woman was old. But was she? Ankylosing Spondilitis, although more common in men is also present in women, and it usually strikes early, when the victim is only a teenager. Perhaps this woman was just eighteen when she first became aware of the disease, and although she had been stooped over for eighteen years, she might not yet have celebrated her fortieth birthday.

Think of it! Bent double so that all she could see were feet and the ground. Not the most dignified of postures. When conquerors wanted to humiliate subjects they made them walk with their backs bowed. One of the most cruel aspects of Ankylosing Spondylitis is that the sufferer cannot walk tall.

Once this unfortunate woman had been a young girl tripping happily with her friends. Once she would have had the dreams common to maturing young women in that culture; dreams of love, home, and children of her own. Then came the illness that changed everything. There is no mention of any friends or family in the story. Was she alone? I wonder when someone last embraced her and gave her a hug to assure her of her worth? It is difficult to hug someone who is bent double. Try it sometime and see for yourself. And eighteen years is a long time to have to walk with your face to the ground.

Does anyone understand this woman as she shuffles along? There are no birds on the wing for her, only feet. No trees, only feet. No faces, only feet. No sun in the sky, only feet. No stars at night, only feet. Her world is one of shadows and gutters. I hope such a child of God will always find love and understanding in church. If worship is to be real and if preaching is to be more than just words *then it must be remembered that there are men and women in attendance at every service who are stooped over mentally, emotionally, and spiritually.*

It is significant that we meet this woman with Ankylosing Spondylitis *in the Synagogue.* I am moved whenever I see anyone who has cause to be angry with God coming to worship him. I think of two dear sisters in their sixties, Kathleen and Margaret. Kathleen was blind and lame. Margaret was deaf, stooped over, and partially sighted. And yet they never missed worship even in the fiercest of weather and their spirits were sweet and serene. They were a testimony to the grace of God.

I understand those so hurt by the bitter blows of life that they turn away from God. I understand but I am saddened. This is just the time when they need Him most. The church is the place for the broken, the hurt, the frightened, the resentful. It is for the people who are so bent by life that they cannot look up and see the sky. If calamity has come to you, if you have found yourself in that dark pit of depression or suffering don't turn your back on God. That is when you need him most. Keep the channels open to receive the wholeness that can come through the life of the spirit so that you too may be enabled to walk tall.

THE ONE FROM WHOM THE HEALING FLOWED—JESUS

Jesus did not give this unfortunate patient advice on how to walk tall; he enabled her to do it. *He had an instinct for sensing someone with need.* It is shared by all who have received His Spirit.

Early in my Christian experience I went one Sunday morning to hear the late Dr. W. E. Sangster at the Central Hall, Westminster. He was considered not only one of the greatest preachers in London but in the whole of England. I little dreamed that this saintly man would become my friend.

After the service, I stood in the vestibule of the Great Hall. There were two exit doors from the auditorium. I chose the one on the right and stood near a nervous little elderly lady who was obviously in distress. Clutching her handbag in one hand she wiped tears from her eyes with the other. By the second exit door a group of foreign diplomats also stood waiting. I found myself contrasting their elegant dress with the shabby appearance of the little lady.

Dr. Sangster chose that morning to come down the aisle leading to the door where the poor elderly lady and I were standing. As I saw him striding purposefully towards the vestibule, I supposed he would go to the group who were obviously important. I was wrong. This distinguished preacher made straight for the little old lady. I see him now as he took her hand and then crouched down in order to make eye contact as he spoke with her. He remained in conversation for several minutes. He seemed oblivious to everyone else. Although I was only twenty years of age, I felt sure the great man was making a mistake and that I knew better. I could see the visiting dignitaries glancing at their watches and whispering to one another. Finally, they left without having spoken to the preacher. "Surely," I thought, "they were the ones who ought to have been receiving most of the attention." Looking back on that scene with the wisdom of the years I now understand. Of course Dr. Sangster had got it right. He instinctively went *to where he was needed most.*

The first call upon the church and its leaders is to go to those whose needs are the most pressing. There is no shortage of those who are eager for the photo opportunities and who can be found where the publicity or the opportunities for self advancement are the greatest. This, however, is not the Jesus way.

Luke does not tell us whether or not there were any important individuals present in the synagogue that day. The one Jesus turned to was the one who needed him most. And we honor and love him for that. Jesus did more than give good advice to that woman in the synagogue. He restored her dignity and self-worth. That is good news!

He touched her. I wonder how long it had been since she had experienced a human touch? There is a therapy in the touch that comes from genuine love and concern. And when he spoke to her we can be certain he would have looked her in the eyes; we cannot imagine Jesus who was all compassion, speaking to the top of her head! *But how would he have made eye contact?* There could be only one way. Like Dr. Sangster, he would have had to go down on one knee and stoop to her. To think that the One we call Lord and Master crouched down in order to look into the eyes of this woman. We must remember of Whom we speak. This is the One of whom Paul would write, "it pleased the Father that in Him should all fullness dwell" (Col. 1:19). Jesus, the Lamb of God who takes away the sins of the world, was kneeling before a poor stooped woman! Heaven would be hushed at such an awesome spectacle.

The greatest blessing conferred on the woman with the bent back in the gospel story was not the ability to look people in the eyes. Marvelous as that was, there was conferred upon her something even more wonderful. She was affirmed to be a daughter of Abraham; a person of unique worth and significance within the plan and purpose of God. She was reminded that she was fashioned in the divine likeness and it was this awareness which enabled her to walk tall even *before* her bent back was cured. The restoration of the container in which her personhood was carried was a bonus.

Each of us is stooped over. No two of us are alike. The cause of our infirmity is unique to each individual. For one it is the result of an emotional trauma. For another it is the consequence of some mental distress. For yet others there are perhaps physical or spiritual factors at work. To each of us Jesus comes. He who is Lord of all stoops to our level and reaches out to touch our infirmity. He gives us the grace to walk tall and be freed from our infirmity. Wholeness begins with inner restoration and it begins now.

Yet a time is coming and has now come
when the true worshippers will worship
the Father in spirit and truth,
for they are the kind of worshippers the Father seeks.
God is spirit, and his worshippers
must worship in spirit and in truth.

JOHN 4:23–24 (NIV)

Chapter Seven

Tapestry, Window, or Door?

June 1995

*P*art of my two years of military service some years after
World War II was spent working as a petroleum
technologist in Singapore. In my unit, the road from the gate
to the adjutant's office was edged by large irregular rocks.
Every morning at 8:00 these rocks would be whitewashed by
men who were confined to barracks for some minor
infraction of military discipline. It was a futile practice
because almost every morning an hour or so later there
would be a brief torrential tropical rainstorm which would
wash every trace of paint away.

One day, just after the rain had stopped, the adjutant
received word that the divisional commander intended to
make a surprise visit within the next hour. Immediately the
unit went to panic stations. The orderly sergeant realized
that the stones needed to be repainted. The soldier who was
at that time confined to barracks was ordered to attend to
the matter. He hurriedly slapped paint on the stones and was
dashing back to the guardroom when, horror of horrors, he
tripped. The can of paint sailed out of his hand and deposited
a glaring pool of white at the main entrance to the unit. My
friend Michael was on duty as orderly sergeant for the last
time before returning to England at the end of the week. He

was quick-witted. He gave orders for the spilled paint to be brushed out into the form of a square about twelve feet wide. It quickly dried under the Singapore sun and by the time the brigadier arrived it looked as though it was an intended part of military decor.

That day I left for duty further north in the Malay peninsula. When I returned two months later the square was still painted. It had joined the curb stones in becoming part of the unit's tradition to be painted each morning and then like them to be washed clean by the torrential rain. No one asked why.

I read about a church in Holland in which the members had a habit of bowing or kneeling before a whitewashed wall in front of the sanctuary before they sat down for worship. The reason for this ritual was unknown. One day the trustees decided to have the whitewashed wall repainted but before doing so they removed the old paint. Underneath they discovered a centuries-old painting of Jesus on the cross. It had been covered up and subsequently lost from memory. The reason for the bowing or kneeling as the congregation entered was forgotten but the practice continued.[1]

What we do in church can easily become a routine, mechanical practice. All of us slip into habits without asking what it is that we are seeking to accomplish. Let us take a closer look at what ought to happen when we come together to worship.

WORSHIP A TAPESTRY—WE COME TO GAZE ON CHRIST

After I was accepted for the Methodist ministry, before going to seminary, I was sent by the conference to be the assistant to one of our outstanding preachers for one year. It was a life-changing experience during which I learned so much.

One of my responsibilities was to speak each Wednesday evening to a large group of members who met in the prayer chapel. No matter how early I arrived, there was someone there before me. She was a lady about sixty years of age. She was a gentle, caring kind of person with tranquillity all about her. I would find her sitting on the front row, her eyes never straying from the cross on the altar.

I subsequently learned that she arrived early because she came directly from the hospital for women in the center of the city. There her daughter was dying. The deaconesses normally visited this hospital but on one occasion I was asked to go. I had never been to such a place before. When I reached the ward I discovered she was in a side room. I was stopped by one of the medical staff. I explained my mission. He was very kind: "Well don't be too long. She tires easily and is only just hanging on. We are expecting to lose her any day." Thanks to skilled medical care she actually lived for another two months. For most of that time she was heavily sedated and barely conscious. Her mother spent hours by her bedside every day. I was amazed at the serenity of this wonderful woman. What heartbreak it must have been for a mother to watch her daughter die in such a lingering fashion!

One morning, cheerfully strolling down the corridor at the church, I happened to meet her as she was coming out of the prayer chapel. I could see that she had been weeping. In my innocent, untutored but well meaning way I asked, "Is there anything I can do?" She smiled bravely and put a motherly hand on my arm. "Nay, lad," she said in her broad Yorkshire accent. "It's all right," and with a glance back into the chapel and at the cross, she added almost in a whisper, "It's been done already." As I came to know her better after her daughter's death, I realized what she meant. Each day she brought her battered and breaking heart to the place of prayer. She did not ask, she did not speak, she just looked.

She rested her mind upon the Lord sitting on the throne of eternity. Heaven cast a light upon her grief and gave her a strange and wonderful peace.

We live in a world where there is much harshness and ugliness. In this past week you have, perhaps, experienced disappointment, discouragement, rejection, or even abuse. A preacher needs to be aware that hiding behind the brave faces in his congregation, there is so very often great pain. The first purpose of worship is to provide an opportunity for us to gaze on Jesus and in gazing, to find comfort and strength. It is a time for unburdening and renewal. In a holy hour we are called to bring our varied talents of music, fellowship, prayer, and preaching and weave a beautiful tapestry to the glory of God. It is a tapestry that reminds us of God's gentle goodness and tender mercy as demonstrated in Christ.

God is spirit and his worshippers must worship in spirit and in truth.

We need to gaze upon the beauty and the goodness of Christ.

Worship a Window—We Have a Vision of Eternity

Can you remember your very first symphony concert? I recall mine vividly. One of the teachers at the high school that I attended took an evangelical approach to music. He was an organist at the local Methodist church and passionate about choral and orchestral works. He took a party of us to the city of Manchester to attend a special concert for school children. The conductor was Sir Malcolm Sargent. In my mind I see him now. He is striding on to the platform, immaculate in his formal black suit, his characteristic white carnation in his lapel. As soon as I cast my eyes on him I was captivated, and the majestic music that he conducted held me spellbound. It was unforgettable. From that moment I was Malcolm Sargent's devoted fan.

Charles Reid in his biography of Sargent compares him with his gifted contemporary Sir Thomas Beecham. In Reid's judgement although Beecham was technically more able, music was for him an end in itself. It could be said that it was a beautiful tapestry and nothing more and the audience was invited to gaze upon it for their enjoyment.[2] Sargent, on the other hand, brought to music his Christian faith and took his audience a step further. He not only wanted his hearers to listen to beautiful sounds. He wanted to take them beyond what they heard to an eternal dimension from which all beauty came. In Reid's judgement, Sargent saw music as a window through which it was possible to see God.

Here is the challenge of worship. Do we bring that sensitivity of spirit that can transform the tapestry into a window? Are we so open to the leading of God's Spirit that we are able to catch a glimpse of heaven?

A returned missionary told of an experience he had when he had just arrived in a remote part of Africa about forty years earlier. An old, venerable African priest was celebrating Holy Communion. The Englishman looked around and noticed that there were only five others present that morning in the service. Afterwards he said to the priest, "Don't you become discouraged when you see so few in your congregation?" The old African looked at the young man and his eyes sparkled. "But did you not see them?" he asked. "See what?" came the reply. "Ah!" exclaimed the old man. "You were not looking with the eyes of the heart. Why! There was a great congregation. There were angels and archangels and all the company of heaven." The missionary said, "I felt chastened. By failing to use the eyes of the heart, I had missed the glory." Then he added, "I am sure it was because of the faithfulness of such saints as the dear old priest that the church there has since grown in such a remarkable way."

When we come to worship, do we use the eyes of the heart? What do we see?

There is a short story by G. W. Target entitled "The Window"[3] which tells of two men, both seriously ill, who occupied the same small hospital room. One man was allowed to sit up in his bed for an hour each afternoon so that fluid could drain from his lungs. His bed was next to the room's only window. The other man had to spend all his time flat on his back.

Every afternoon when the man in the bed by the window could sit up, he would describe to his roommate all the things he could see outside the window. The man in the other bed began to live for those moments when the outside world with its life and color was described for him. The window overlooked a park with a lovely lake, the man said. Ducks and swans played on the water while children sailed their model boats. Lovers walked arm in arm amid flowers of every color of the rainbow. Grand old trees graced the landscape, and a fine view of the city skyline could be seen in the distance. As the man by the window described all this in exquisite detail, the man on the other side of the room would close his eyes and imagine the picturesque scene.

One warm afternoon, the man by the window described a parade passing by. Although the other man couldn't hear the band, he could see it in his mind's eye. Then unexpectedly, an alien thought entered his head. "Why should he have all the pleasure of seeing everything while I never get to see anything?" It didn't seem fair.

Gradually envy turned to bitter resentment. He began to brood and he found himself unable to sleep. *He* should be by that window—that thought now controlled his life. Late one night, as he lay staring at the ceiling, the man by the window began to cough. He was choking because of the fluid in his lungs. The other man watched in the dimly lit room as the struggling man by the window groped for the button to call for help. Though able, he never moved to push his own button that would have brought the nurse running. In less than five minutes the coughing and choking stopped, along with the sound of breathing. Now there was only silence—deathly silence.

The following morning the day nurse arrived to find the lifeless body of the man by the window. She was saddened and called the hospital attendants to take him away—no words, no fuss. When it seemed appropriate, the other man asked if he could be moved next to the window. The nurse was happy to make the switch, and after making sure he was comfortable, she left him alone. Slowly, painfully, he propped himself up on one elbow to take his first look. Finally, he would have the joy of seeing it all himself. He strained to look out the window beside the bed. It faced a blank wall.

That can happen in worship when we do not use the eyes of the heart. Oh, of course, the wall, or tapestry, is beautiful. It lifts the spirit and brings a sense of peace, but there is so much more that it can do. To those with eyes to see, the tapestry or wall is transformed into a window. It is no longer an end in itself but a means by which we see into the mystery of God and the purpose of life—and this is a transforming experience.

Worship a Door—We Find Christ

Worship has not, however, completely fulfilled its purpose when it has presented us with a lovely tapestry on which to gaze or has become a window through which we glimpse the glory of eternity. There yet remains a third dimension. Worship can and must do more. It can become a door through which we enter into a personal relationship with God in Christ.

In the annals of one of England's great city missions there is a treasured story of a poor woman who was in deep distress. During a time of economic depression she and her husband had moved in search of work. They had only been in their new location five weeks when fever swept through the neighborhood and her husband was one of its first casualties. She was left with five children, desolated, lonely, and isolated. She was a stranger in the community and without a friend to whom she could turn.

Shortly after her husband's funeral she returned from a stall in the market where she had been to buy some vegetables. The vendor had wrapped them in an old newspaper for her. Back home in her kitchen she noticed an article in the newspaper. It told of remarkable things happening in the city twelve miles away under the ministry of a Methodist named Samuel Collier. The report said, "Not a week goes by without men and women finding Christ in Mr. Collier's services." As she read the article, memories of her childhood were stirred. She thought about the Sunday School which she attended with her parents and remembered their simple faith. In her grief and loneliness she yearned to know Christ as they had.

She had not been to church for many years. She had no Sunday clothes. She did not even possess a pair of shoes and wore the wooden clogs common amongst the poor of her day. The following Sunday morning, however, she set off for church. She put her oldest child in charge of four younger ones and then walked the twelve miles in her clogs to the place where Samuel Collier was to preach.

The congregation was assembling as she arrived. She noticed how fashionably they were dressed, and she became conscious of her own shabby appearance. Overcoming her sense of embarrassment, she bravely walked up the steps to the door. An usher smiled in greeting paying no attention to her humble appearance and treating her as graciously as he did everyone else. He gave her a warm word of welcome and offered her a hymnal. She took it, and, encouraged by his kind greeting, blurted out, "Excuse me sir, but is this the place where I can find Christ?" The man appeared to be deeply moved. He gently took her arm and led her into the church to a pew. He whispered "Sit here my dear. This is where my wife and I usually sit. Before the service is over, if you are really serious, Christ will come to you. You see," he added with misty eyes, "this is where he came to me just three months ago."

If that woman in her clogs had come to you or me this morning and asked, "Is this the place where I can find Jesus," what would we have said?

What is worship? A beautiful tapestry gladdening the senses? Yes. A window opening up the wonders of heaven? Yes. A door through which we pass into a personal encounter with Christ? Oh, please God, yes!

Listen! Can you hear a gentle, quiet, insistent knocking? In worship, if you listen particularly carefully you will hear a voice whispering, "I stand at the door and knock; if anyone hears my voice and opens the door, I will come in and eat with him and he with me."

As he approached Jerusalem and saw the city,

he wept over it and said,

"If you, even you, had only known on this day

what would bring you peace—

but now it is hidden from your eyes. . . .

because you did not recognize the time

of God's coming to you."

LUKE 19:41–44 (NIV)

I Wonder What He Saw?

July 1997

I wonder what Jesus saw? Why the tears?

My friend Dolph Smith is an artist who paints in water-colors. He retired quite recently after thirty years of teaching from an art college in Memphis. We visited him in the lovely home that he has built overlooking a beautiful hilly landscape just out of town. On part of the land that he has inherited is an old barn, badly in need of repair and yet having a rustic charm. Dolph told me how he developed the urge to capture that charm on canvas. He thought that with the backdrop of the hills, it could make a powerful picture, evocative of bygone times when people were not in such a great rush.

One sunny day he set off with a picnic lunch and his case of painting materials. He took with him a little folding table that he erected once he had reached a convenient vantage point. He carefully arranged his small jars of water paint on it, then his brushes and his pallet. Before getting out his easel and canvas he sat and allowed his artistic mind to mull over the scene, waiting for a visitation from the creative muses.

Just then an old farmer passed by on a tractor. Unaccustomed to seeing anyone in that particular spot, he stopped, climbed down, and approached Dolph. My friend, wrapped in creative contemplation, did not hear him. The old farmer came up and took in the scene. He could see a stranger gazing across the field at the old barn. Beside him was the small table on which were neatly arranged little pots of paint together with several brushes. Eventually the farmer's curiosity got the better of him. Breaking into the artist's reverie he asked, "What are you fixin' to do?" Dolph looked up, smiled, and pointed to the barn. "I'm fixing to paint that barn," he said. The farmer slowly absorbed what the stranger had said. He stood in silence taking another long hard look at the small jars of paint on the table. Then his eyes shifted to the large dilapidated barn. After a pause for reflection he scratched his head and said very slowly in a note of incredulity, "Are you fixin' to paint *all* of it?"

The farmer saw only some small jars of paint and a large old barn. In his mind the one was not adequate to the needs of the other. He lived in a world of material things. The artist however did not just see a barn. He saw a picture. He lived in a world of vision. Which of these two saw more?

When I was the general manager of one of England's district health authorities, an assistant called my attention to a poem published in the *Health Service Journal* of December 18, 1986. The poem has travelled far since it first appeared. The author was an old lady called Kate who died in Napsbury Hospital, St. Albans, Hertfordshire. She was unable to speak but was occasionally known to write. After her death, her locker was emptied and the poem found. It is entitled "What Do You See?" In the poem, she is addressing this question to the nurses who are looking after her and who do not realize that the old lady is taking in everything they say and do. She goes on:

Then open your eyes, nurse, you're not looking at me
As I'll tell you who I am, as I sit here so still,
As I rise at your bidding as I eat at your will.

I'm a small child of ten with a mother and father,
Brothers and sisters who love one another.

Now a girl of sixteen with wings on her feet,
Dreaming that soon now, a lover she'll meet.

A bride soon at twenty; my heart gives a leap
Remembering the vows that I promised to keep.

At twenty-five now I have young of my own
Who need me to build a secure, happy home.

A young woman of thirty, my young now grow fast,
Bound to each other with ties that should last

At forty, my young ones, now grown will soon be gone
But my man stays beside me, to see I don't mourn.

At fifty once more, babies play round my knee.
Again we know children, my loved one and me.

Dark days are upon me, my husband is dead
I look to the future, I shudder with dread,
For my young are all busy rearing young of their own,
And I think of the years and the love I have known.

I'm an old woman now, and nature is cruel
'Tis her jest to make old age to look like a fool
But inside this old carcass, a young girl still dwells

And now and again my battered heart swells.
I remember the joys, I remember the pain,
And I'm loving and living life over again.

So open your eyes, nurses, open and see
Not a crabbit old woman; look closer . . . see ME.

I wonder what Jesus saw?

As the disciples approached the city and looked down on the gleaming towers of Jerusalem they cheered with excited delight. What did they see? They saw the city which, they thought, was about to crown their leader king. When Jesus looked down at Jerusalem, Luke 19:41 tells us that he who was the most joyful of men wept. Wept! We speak of crying. When we want to give the emotion emphasis we talk about bursting into tears. But there is something about that old word "weep" that introduces a note of passion. The Greek word Luke uses here is far stronger than the one John 11:35 uses to describe the tears at the grave of Lazarus. It expresses deep anguish. Jesus sobbed violently. Why? What did he see? Why the tears?

TEARS OF GRIEF

Young, healthy, grown men don't weep. Such a thing is considered unmanly in our culture. A stiff upper lip is what is expected. In extreme old age, exhaustion, and sickness, it may be permissible for a man to shed tears, but not otherwise. We furtively wipe our eyes when deeply moved by a film or a sermon, embarrassed by such a show of weakness. But I have seen a grown man weep. He was an obstetrician. The baby was stillborn with the cord around its neck. He had been called too late. There was nothing he could do. The mother was a close friend of his. She and her husband had longed for a baby for twelve years. Overwhelmed, that strong young man wept. He shed tears of grief.

I have seen a grown man weep. He was a policeman. A young mother was driving her car down a quiet country lane with her two children in the back. A large truck that had no business coming down that road and certainly not at that speed appeared suddenly from a hidden bend heading straight for her. The collision was unavoidable. The "bobby" sat in the emergency room as the mother and the surviving child were taken to intensive care. Nothing could be done for the youngest one. When he heard the news, that young strong police officer, who had seen a great deal of roadside carnage, wept. He shed tears of grief.

Before Jesus stretches the city he loves, Jerusalem. There are children playing in its streets. He can hear their laughter and their excited chatter. Men and women are strolling out together. Families are gathering for the great annual celebration of Passover. It is a time of festivity. It is both a solemn and a joyful festival. There would be an atmosphere rather similar to that which envelopes us at Christmas. Jesus looks across the city and sees, hidden below all its bustle and activity, human stories of heart-break, pain, and unfulfilled dreams. He sees lives that have never reached their full potential. He sees the terrible suffering that is in store for it because of the shortsightedness of its leaders. And he who was so full of joy, the life and soul of every party, breaks down and weeps tears of grief. "*O Jerusalem, Jerusalem, if thou hadst known. . . .*" Others saw only the city and shouted with joy. Jesus saw it *all* and wept.

He comes again in our day and looks over our towns and cities. He sees us struggling with ill health, with fears and anxieties, with hidden personal difficulties. He sees the pain which we create for ourselves by our selfishness. He takes it all upon himself and weeps tears of grief for the hurts that are ours.

TEARS OF SHAME

We have all experienced the kind of shame that is really a veiled sort of embarrassment. Charles Swindall in *Simple Faith*[1] tells of a traveller who, between flights at an airport, bought a small package of cookies. She then sat down in the busy snack shop to glance over the newspaper. As she read her paper, she became aware of a rustling noise. Peeping over the newsprint she was shocked to see a well-dressed gentleman sitting across from her, helping himself to her cookies. Half-angry and half-embarrassed she reached over and gently slid the package closer to her as she took one out and began to munch on it. A minute or so passed before she heard more rustling. The man had taken another cookie! By now there was only one left in the package. Though flabbergasted, she didn't want to make a scene so she said nothing. Finally, as if to add insult to injury, the man broke the remaining cookie into two pieces, pushed one piece across the table toward her with a frown, gulped down his half, and left without even saying thank you.

The woman sat there dumbfounded. Some time later when her flight was announced, she opened her handbag to get her ticket. To her embarrassment and dismay, there in her purse was her package of unopened cookies. Somewhere in that same airport was another traveller trying to figure out how that strange woman could have been so forward and insensitive. Imagine the shame that she must have felt.

There is, however, a deeper kind of shame. Some years ago I was the visiting preacher at a certain church in England. Just before the service one of the laymen, a man known for his genuine goodness and Christian grace, asked if he could have a few minutes of my time after the service. When the congregation had gone, he and I met in a side room. He was in deep torment as he unburdened himself. "I just had to talk to someone," he said. "It is about our middle son. My other two boys have always been high achievers and they are both in splendid jobs and with lovely families. Our middle one was always the odd one out. We think he suffered from cerebral anoxia at birth. He was always very slow. He was not sufficiently retarded to warrant special education and attended the regular school. I think that is where his problem began. Unlike his two brothers, his school record was one of abysmal failure. There was no consolation in sports and athletics; he hated them.

"He was a gullible boy easily led. He made the wrong kind of friends who led him astray. We tried so hard to understand and help, but eventually he walked out and went off with two of this gang to the coast. He broke off all contact with us, and I know he stopped going to church. We tried every way you can think of to regain contact but he blocked us at every point. All that was over fifteen years ago. Last week we heard that the three of them had been arrested. They have admitted the charge," and here the man swallowed, and looked away. "I am so deeply ashamed," he said. "Deeply ashamed." As I listened to the man, I realized what was happening. He had taken upon himself the guilt and the shame of his son. It was as though he had committed the offenses himself.

Jesus comes and looks upon the city. He sees its sordidness, its callous indifference to need, its hypocrisy, and its lust. In a profound and mystical way, he takes all this upon himself and weeps with shame. In a similar way, he looks upon our lives with our sins and shortcomings and makes them his own. He weeps for us and they are tears of shame.

If Jesus is weeping because of the shortcomings in our lives then why aren't we? The closer we are to him, the more we are overwhelmed by shame. This shame is not only for our own sins but also for the sins of the society of which we are part. A Christian from the Indian subcontinent wrote a lovely hymn which has in it this verse:

So, Love itself in human form,
For love of me He came;
I cannot look upon His face
For shame, for bitter shame.

TEARS OF FRUSTRATION

When I was about twelve years old, I was introduced to the game of Monopoly by a wealthy friend at school. The game then cost five shillings (about fifty cents) and seemed utterly beyond my limited means. Then my fortune changed. That summer, my parents decided I could follow in my older brother's footsteps and help in gathering the harvest on one of the neighboring farms.

I was given a job by Mr. Dandy. He paid three pence an hour, and that was slightly better than the going rate. A quick calculation—eight hours each day for five days — meant that by Friday night I would receive one hundred and twenty pence. In our old English coinage that was equal to ten shillings. It had become the custom in our family—

which we happily accepted without question—that when one of the children obtained any part-time job, half of what was earned could be kept. The balance then went into the meager family treasury. By the end of the week, therefore, five shillings would be mine. The exact price for the game of Monopoly! A dream was about to come true! Throughout that week as I worked with other boys in the wheat field gathering the sheaves, my mind was dominated by just one thought: Monopoly.

On Friday night, we all filed past Mr. Dandy. A genial avuncular man, he was seated behind a little table on which was placed a cash tin. From it he handed to each boy what I then considered to be one of the most beautiful things in all the world—a brown crisp new ten-shilling note. I had never held so much money of my own in my hand before.

I waited at the bus stop, holding my bank note and thinking about the following morning when I would go to buy the game of Monopoly. The bus arrived, and I brought out my penny for the fare and, with my mind far away, took the ticket and floated to my seat. I was thinking of Saturday afternoon and a Monopoly party at our house. Would I invite Roy and Claude to join my brothers and me? Would I be the banker? Still in a reverie the bus reached my stop. I got up and made my way to the exit, my mind on the game of Monopoly. Dreamily, I got off the bus, putting my ticket in the used ticket box at the entrance to the bus, and sauntered down the road home clutching my bank note and thinking of Monopoly.

I wandered into the house to receive the usual warm welcome from my mother. The first thing I did was to hand her the ten-shilling note. To her surprise and my dismay what I gave her was my bus ticket! My ten-shilling note was in the used ticket box of the bus! I had mixed them up.

Without thinking of a meal, my older brother and I got our bicycles out and we pedaled furiously after the bus, knowing that it had a thirty-minute break at the terminal just a mile away. We arrived panting for breath to find the driver and conductor having a cup of tea and a cigarette. Frantically, we told our story. The conductor, who had boys of his own, smiled and said "Well let's have a look shall we?" He opened the flap at the bottom of the used ticket box and there amongst all the tickets we saw it, the most beautiful sight in all the world, a brown ten-shilling note. We showered the kind man with our profuse thanks and returned home guarding that precious note as if it were the crown jewels.

I had taken my eye off the real treasure and finished up clasping something utterly worthless. That was the story of the Jerusalem over which Jesus looked. Centuries earlier God, who had all the people of earth from which to choose, selected a group of homeless slaves and called them to a special mission. They were to be "a special treasure," the divinely appointed servants to take a message of mercy and grace to the world. Instead of being God's instrument for saving others, however, the people had become obsessed by inward-looking, narrow-minded politics. They had exchanged the priceless treasure of servanthood for doomed nationalism. As Jesus looked across the city and saw how God's purpose for the nation was being thwarted, he wept and his tears were tears of frustration.

What about the church today? When I was a young preacher I often used to see in the country pulpits a message printed on a card and pinned where only the preacher's eye would notice it. The words of the message were the words of the Greeks to the disciples: "Sir, we would see Jesus." It was a silent reminder that the chief end of preaching is the sharing of Christ with others. This is the task of the whole people of God. There is nothing more important.

As the Savior looks at we who are the church, I wonder what He sees? Does He see the church true to its mission? Does He see her spending herself in loving obedient service to all? Does He see her guarding the faith once delivered to the saints and preserving it untarnished in an age of compromise? Oh may this be so! For then, mingled with his sorrow, will also be tears of joy.

The Lord is my shepherd,
I shall not want.
He makes me lie down in green pastures;
he leads me beside still waters; he restores my soul.

PSALM 23:1–3 (NRSV)

I am the good shepherd . . .
and I lay down my life for the sheep.

JOHN 10:14–15 (NRSV)

Chapter Nine

The Genuine Article

August 1995

Many years ago a preacher said something one Sunday morning that made an indelible impression on my mind. Edward Rogers came as a visitor to my home church to take part in its centenary celebrations. He was a scholarly man with an unusual staccato delivery and a dry sense of humor that had an immediate appeal. He subsequently became one of the most distinguished ministers of the British Conference.

His theme that morning was "The Manhood of the Master" and he set out to describe a robust, vigorous, thoroughly vibrant Savior. "I used to have a problem with the idea of Jesus as the Good Shepherd," he said, "because my mind was filled with pictures of an effete figure holding little lambs and looking as though a breeze would blow him over." He then went on to tell of an event in his ministry that changed all that.

During the latter part of World War II he was invited to preach at a rural church in the south of England and to stay for lunch with a local sheep farmer and his family. In 1940 the Air Ministry had requisitioned part of the farmer's land because it was a level pasture and was needed as an emergency landing field by the Royal Air Force. The pasture was surrounded by coils of barbed wire and guarded. During August and September of that year, fighter planes used it in the Battle of Britain when the fate of the nation rested on the courage of our airmen. Later, as the tide of war turned, this landing field was no longer required and the service personnel were moved elsewhere. The Air Ministry, however, still held on to it and it seemed to be forgotten.

Neglected, the landing field reverted back to nature. The grass, no longer cropped short, grew until it was almost waist high and the barbed wire was hidden from view. From time to time the sheep grazing in the neighboring fields would be enticed by the promise of richer pasture and unmindful of the danger would stumble into the wire and become entangled.

Edward Rogers told us how on this particular Sunday as he and the family were just about to begin lunch there was a loud knocking at the front door. It was one of the farmer's neighbors. "Quick," the neighbor cried, "Your sheep are in the wire." It was obvious that this was a fairly common emergency to which the family was accustomed. As if on cue they all immediately rose from the table and rushed out to rescue the sheep. Edward Rogers confessed that, wearing a clerical collar, he could not sit idly by so he reluctantly offered his services. He was assigned one part of the field and as he went amongst this high grass, searching for sheep he said dryly, "I was unlucky, I found one!" He struggled to extricate it from the barbed wire as the terrified animal wrestled with him. Eventually, he finished up with the sheep in his arms, although he confessed that he was not sure whether he was carrying the sheep or the sheep was carrying him. Just then, the farmer arrived on the scene. "Here, let me have that sheep Mr. Rogers," he said. Rogers then told us how the farmer, a big, strong man, his sleeves rolled up, arms lacerated and bleeding from encounters with barbed wire, took hold of the front paws of the sheep in one big fist and the rear paws in the other. He then slung the sheep on his back like a sack of coal and carried it to safety. The preacher concluded, "Now when I think about the good shepherd, I see that strong man, his arms torn and bleeding, carrying that stupid, struggling, frightened creature from danger to safety."

The image of the shepherd is a recurring one in Scripture. David speaks of God, the Eternal, the Holy One as being his shepherd. What a breathtaking claim! The prophets speak of the Almighty as one who will feed the flock like a shepherd. Those who were called to leadership of God's people in the Old Testament were considered metaphorically as shepherds and their failings provoked the prophet Ezekiel to launch a fierce attack on them. "Therefore, you shepherds, hear the word of the Lord . . . I am against the shepherds and will hold them accountable for my flock." He adds, "I myself will tend my sheep and have them lie down, declares the Sovereign Lord. I will search for the lost and bring back the strays . . . I will shepherd the flock with justice" (Ezek. 34:7–16).

In the fullness of time there came One who fulfilled the promise declared by Ezekiel. Jesus said "I am the good shepherd and I lay down my life for the sheep."

A PICTURE OF GOD IN CHRIST AS A GENUINE SHEPHERD

I have only ever bought one diamond. The occasion was my engagement. It was unforgettable for a number of reasons. One of them was the necessity to sell my dearly beloved motorcycle in order to raise the necessary funds. The jeweller was a member of the church in which my fiancée and

I grew up and we were good friends. I, therefore, felt able to be frank and honest with him. "Tell me, Norman," I said, looking at the small ring and thinking of my late lamented motorcycle, "can anyone other than an expert really tell the difference between this ring and those cheap imitations in Woolworth's across the road? To me they all look alike." Norman smiled patiently and disappeared into the back room. He returned with another ring. "This one, Reg, is an imitation," he said. "Just compare it with the real thing." With that, he switched on a bright light above the counter and handed me his jeweler's eyepiece. I compared the two. In my left hand was the counterfeit. In my right was the genuine article, the one that had cost me a motorcycle. Superficially they looked alike, but when placed side by side under that searching scrutiny, there was no comparison. The genuine diamond flashed with brilliance and scintillated with life and light. By its side, the counterfeit was a dull lusterless thing.

In John 10:11–15, Jesus describes two men in the sheep business. They are both similar in appearance. Their faces are bronzed by their outdoor life. They wear similar clothes and each has hanging from his belt a club or rod. In the hand of each is a shepherd's crook. One of these is only a hireling, the other is the genuine article, a true shepherd. The first is there because he is paid for his work. His dedication reaches no further than his purse. He has a shepherd's crook but not a shepherd's heart. In normal times this hireling has us completely fooled. He does not make a bad job of looking after the sheep; he counts and feeds them and prevents them from straying. But when there is a moment of testing as when a wolf makes a menacing appearance it is a very different story. Then the hireling is weighed in the balances and found wanting. He does the most natural thing in the world, he runs to save himself. He is not going to stay around and get hurt. He is being paid to look after sheep not to be torn apart by wolves. The true shepherd, however, stays. The safety of his sheep comes before his own, even though it cost him his life.

Jesus is the genuine shepherd, and he demonstrates how far he will go to protect us stubborn, willful wandering sheep by laying down his life for us. It is fitting that the shepherd image should be in the mind of the church whenever Christian service is considered. I remember how moved and challenged I was when, at my ordination, we sang some words by Charles Wesley:

Jesus, Thy wandering sheep behold!
See, Lord, with tenderest pity see
The sheep that cannot find the fold,
Till sought and gathered in by Thee.

Thou, only Thou, the kind and good
And sheep-redeeming Shepherd art:
Collect Thy flock, and give them food,
And pastors after Thine own heart.

What higher calling can there be than to share in the ministry of the One true genuine shepherd? This is our holy vocation, to be like Christ, to care for others not because there is something in it for us, but because we have loving hearts. We, like Jesus, are called to be the genuine article.

A Picture of God in Christ as a Personal Shepherd

"The heart of religion," said Luther, "lies in its personal pronouns." What did he mean by that? He was affirming that faith is not a question of intellectual knowledge like knowing the composition of a particular compound or the rock structure of some distant land. It is a personal experience, something that we have made our own in our minds and hearts. The New Testament writers continually return to the first person pronouns *my*, *we*, and *our*. Paul writes to the Galatian Christians, "I have been crucified with Christ and I no longer live, but Christ lives in me" (Gal. 2:20 [NIV]). At the beginning of his first letter, John says, "We have heard . . . we have seen with our eyes . . . our hands have touched" (1 John 1:1–2). The great confession of Thomas that is in many ways the climax of the fourth gospel is so powerful because of the pronouns "*My* Lord and *my* God!" (John 20:28). One of the arresting features in the writings of the Wesleys is the use of the pronoun *my*. In one of his powerful hymns on the theme of the cross, Charles Wesley wrote:

> *O love divine, what hast though done!*
> *The immortal God hath died for me!*
> *The Father's co-eternal Son*
> *Bore all my sins upon the tree.*
> *The immortal God for me hath died,*
> My *Lord*, my *Love is crucified.*

When his brother John recorded his life-changing heart-warming experience at Aldersgate Street, he wrote, "I felt that I did believe in Christ, Christ alone for salvation and an assurance was given *me* that He had taken away *my* sins, even *mine* and saved *me* from the law of sin and death." This discovery that in all the circumstances of our lives God is not just "a shepherd" but *my* shepherd lies at the heart of evangelical Christianity.

As I read the Twenty-third Psalm, I find myself asking, "Did this awareness that God was his personal shepherd came to David gradually or did it burst upon him with sudden breathtaking wonder?"

During my final year as a medical student, the intern who was working on the diabetic unit in the General Hospital was involved in an accident. I was asked by the professor to substitute for him until he was able to resume his duties. As a result, in the following ten weeks I learned more about the extremes in diabetes than could have been gleaned from a hundred textbooks. During my second night on duty in the diabetic unit, a lady was admitted in a deep hypoglycemic coma. I was called to the Emergency Room. Of course I knew the treatment; it is a standard procedure. Intravenous glucose solution has to be administered immediately. Under the watchful eye of the senior resident, I inserted the needle of the syringe into a vein in the patient's arm and slowly began the infusion. I had read about the dramatic effect of this treatment. I had heard about it from my tutors. But what happened was beyond my expectations. Almost before I had finished the injection, the patient had opened her eyes and smiled. I felt a sudden overwhelming feeling of elation. Yes, it was true! It really worked! My teachers were right. The textbooks were sound. At that moment, I could believe the story about the Greek philosopher Archimedes. The legend is that, lying in his bath, the principles of flotation and displacement suddenly came to him. He was so excited, it is said, that he leapt from his bath and rushed naked down the streets of Athens crying "Eureka"—I have found it!

Christian history is full of stories of those who in a dark night of the soul have suddenly been overwhelmed by the realization that God is a tender personal shepherd, and they could say, "All that God is, is mine." For others, this glorious realization has not come suddenly. For them it has dawned gradually, and they have slowly responded to the love of God as a flower opens to the sun. They may not be able to give a time or a place but they *know*. Whether this awareness has come suddenly or gradually is unimportant. What matters is that each of us is able to affirm at this moment that we know God to be a personal shepherd and in the deep places of our being we are absolutely sure we are not just part of a long impersonal cosmic list but are individually known. As Jesus put it, "The hairs of our heads are all numbered."

During my term as its minister, a large church in the north of England celebrated its fiftieth anniversary. To mark this Golden Jubilee one of the members decided to raise money to purchase new banners for the sanctuary. What she did was not startlingly novel. She made a large tablecloth and at its center embroidered a sketch of the church. She then invited the staff and members to sign their names on pieces of paper and make a contribution to her "fund." Hundreds responded and all the signatures were sewn into the tablecloth in a variety of colors. We wondered what she planned to do with the finished work. This remained a secret until the service at which my wife and I bade farewell to this congregation we had come to love. In a very moving moment we were presented with the tablecloth as a token of remembrance. We were overwhelmed and it is now one of our most treasured possessions. We bring it out to use on special occasions and once again we see the names of some of the splendid men and women we knew; we remember their hopes, their laughter, their anxieties, and their tears. They are not just names. The tablecloth is more than a list. Each one is a person and has a special place in our hearts and affections.

Maud's name is there. Maud was a lovely soul. She was a devoted founder member of that church. She lived in one of the poor areas of the city. Her old cottage still required the use of a coin gas meter. These have long since disappeared but at that time some persisted in some older houses. Each meter was equipped with a knob and a slot for a shilling coin. It was a method of prepayment for a supply of gas. When the shilling was inserted the knob had to be turned, pushing the coin into a locked collecting box. Then the appropriate measure of gas was delivered. Maud had to do this three or four times a week. Once a month an official from the gas company would come to unlock the meter and collect the money. Unfortunately, Maud's meter was faulty and she had to shake it in order to make the shilling fall so that the gas supply could be triggered. She did not mention this problem to the collector when he made his monthly visits. She knew nothing about metal fatigue and did not realize what the years of shaking were doing to the lead gas pipe connected to the meter. One Thursday morning I was summoned by the police to Maud's home. Anxious neighbors had not heard her moving about and the milk had not been collected from the doorstep. With a young police constable I broke into the little cottage to find her lying quite still in her armchair. She had been overcome by gas leaking from the fractured gas pipe. Maud's name is on the tablecloth. It's not just a name, it's a person whom I knew, with whom I prayed, and for whom I grieved.

Every single sheep is known. Some are self-effacing little people who snatch no headlines and make no great stir. The world does not know its greatest men and women and the church does not know its best. We are in for some surprises in heaven. Well has it been said that "the healing of the world is in its nameless saints." The Captain of the host has many unknown soldiers, loyal and brave who wear no decorations, are never mentioned in dispatches, who depart without any wailing bugle. The first trumpets they ever hear are those saluting them on the other side of the river—but after all, those are the only ones that really matter. The world may not know them but the Savior has their names graven on the palms of his hands for He is a personal shepherd.

A PICTURE OF GOD IN CHRIST AS A SEEKING SHEPHERD

David says of the great Shepherd, "He restores my soul." This word *restore* comes from the Hebrew word *Shub* that means *to turn back*. I like the translation, "He brings me back again from wandering."

William Barclay writing about the parable of the lost sheep tells us that Galilean shepherds were experts at tracking and could follow the straying sheep's footprints for miles across the hills. He adds that many of the flocks were communal, belonging not to individuals but to villages. There would be two or three shepherds in charge. Those whose flocks were safe would arrive home on time, and they would bring news if one shepherd were still out on the mountain side searching for a sheep that was lost. The whole village would be on the watch, and when in the distance they saw the shepherd striding home with the lost sheep across his shoulders there would rise from the whole community a shout of joy and thanksgiving. And Jesus said, "God is like that, as glad when a lost sinner is found as a shepherd bringing a strayed sheep home."

King David wandered. There was a dark period in his life when God was far from his thoughts and actions and he behaved very differently to the young man he was when he wrote about the Shepherd God. Few figures in the Bible sinned so greatly, yet David is remembered with affection and admiration. He stands tall because although he wandered, he was willing to repent and be brought back home.

I was the visiting preacher at a church in the south of England several years ago. At the end of the evening service, I stood at the door bidding farewell to the congregation. As one by one they filed out, I noticed a man hovering in the background. He waited until the last person had left and then he came and grasped my hand. He stood looking into my face with a sad, haunted expression evidently searching for words. He mumbled a brief appreciation for the service then added in a wistful way, "You know, five years ago I was in your position." I looked questioningly, and he continued, "I was a minister in another denomination and in another town. I had the church of my dreams, but I threw it all away. I wandered a long way." He paused, choked with emotion, then added, "I only came here tonight on impulse." I replied, "No matter how far you have wandered, there is always a way back." He shook his head and said emphatically. "No. It's a long story, but there's no way back for me." With that he was down the church steps and gone. I hurried after him, but he had disappeared into the November mist. I called after him hoping that he would give me a little more time, but he did not return. "Who was that man?" I asked the church stewards. They shook their heads; they had never seen him before.

I have no idea what it was that caused that stranger to feel that he had wandered too far. Despite the passage of years, his face still haunts me because he was so wrong. Although overwhelmed by remorse, regret, and guilt, he was wrong. None of us can wander beyond the love and mercy of God. The penitent is always welcomed by the seeking Shepherd who never gives up on us. It is not too late to hear his voice.

In a world of uncertainty, pain, and fear, the Genuine Article, the true Good Shepherd shines before us as the One who truly cares, who knows us by name, and who never gives up on us. The sad truth is that some of us are foolish enough to give up on Him!

Like an eagle that stirs up its nest
and hovers over its young,
that spreads its wings to catch them
and carries them on its pinions.
The Lord alone did lead him; [Israel].

DEUTERONOMY 32:11–12 (NIV)

The eternal God is your refuge,
and underneath are the everlasting arms.

DEUTERONOMY 33:27 (NIV)

Chapter Ten

Providential Disturbance

August 1998

*A*s a teenager I attended an evangelistic youth rally in my hometown. The speaker in that crowded YMCA building was an officer in the Royal Navy. He held his audience spellbound with stirring accounts of answered prayer during World War II. The story with the greatest impact came from his experience when on destroyer duty escorting convoys to Russia. This was considered to be one of the most dangerous assignments of the British Home Fleet. The route took the ships to the far west and north of the coast of Norway, through the arctic Barents Sea and finally to the Russian port of Murmansk. Underneath the perilous icy waters lurked the menace of enemy submarines.

The speaker told us how, just before his ship left port to escort another convoy, he developed appendicitis. He was immediately transferred to hospital and another officer was called from leave to take his place. The convoy ran into a pack of submarines off the northern coast of Norway. The destroyer shield immediately went into action to protect the freighters. The ship on which he would have been serving was hit by a torpedo. Amongst those who were killed was the officer who had taken his place. "I stand before you tonight," the speaker said "As a living testimony to the providence of God. Far from being a misfortune, my appendicitis was a blessing. God sent it in order to protect me."

I have heard that kind of testimony for the past forty years. I have heard it in all parts of the world. I have heard it about families, about businesses, about illness, about tragedy. In every case the speakers have been perfectly sincere. Their motives have been beyond reproach. They were affirming their gratitude to God for blessings received. I want to say, however, as gently as I know how, that I find this kind of testimony a problem. It troubled me at that YMCA meeting as a teenager and it troubles me still. What do we mean by "providence?" Is it just another name for getting our own way and having things go right for us? What about the man who was called back from leave and sailed with the convoy to his death because our speaker developed appendicitis? Where was providence for him?

In examining this perplexing subject I turn to words of Moses in his farewell address recorded in the book of Deuteronomy. For forty years he has led his people through the wilderness. He has shared their heartbreaks, joys, disappointments, and triumphs. Searching for a description of God's care he offers an arresting analogy. God, he says, *is like an eagle.*

The eagles seek out a sheltered ledge on the mountainside. Stick by stick they make their nest strong and sure. The female lines it with feathers from her own breast. She ensures that her helpless young will lack for nothing. Secure, the newly hatched chicks lie in the nest with nothing to worry about. They have parents who protect and feed them as they grow. It is a snug, comfortable, carefree life. They do not want to be disturbed. Then, one day, the parent eagles swoop down on the ledge, but this time not bearing food. Instead they begin to tear the nest to pieces, scattering it in all directions. The little eaglets are left trembling on the bare ledge exposed to the cruel elements.

This is not a case of parents losing their temper. This is an act of mercy. These eaglets must learn to fly if they are to survive and that cannot happen if they stay in the nest. They stand on the perilous ledge watching their parents taking off and soaring into the sky. Eventually one of them, a little braver than the others, takes the plunge. He opens his untried wings and tries to fly. Then he falters and, paralyzed with fear, he begins to fall. Suddenly one of the parents swoops down underneath the falling eaglet and bears him up on his strong pinions back to the ledge again. It is as though the parents are saying "You failed that time; but we were watching. Keep on trying until your wings are strong enough. Trust us. We shall be there if you fall."

The eaglets had a higher destiny than just sleeping and eating. They were destined for the sky and to achieve their full potential they needed to be stirred out of their complacency. *The same love that made the nest had to destroy it.* In truly caring for its young the eagle must disturb them. This is why Moses saw the monarch of the skies as offering a glimpse into the mystery of divine providence.

PROVIDENCE—LIKE THE EAGLE—
A DISTURBING PROVIDER

One place in American homes that I always enjoy is the refrigerator door. It has a lot to tell about those who live there. This is where you can see all kinds of family stuff such as cartoons featuring Snoopy, memos about church activities, reminders about soccer games, dental appointments, and drawings by children.

Years ago, on one of our early visits to the United States, my wife and I were being shown round a lovely home in a small town. On the refrigerator door was a large picture of a flashy sports car taken from a magazine. "That's what our son is praying for," said the proud father. "Every time he comes for a snack between meals he gives it a pat and offers up a prayer for it. We are all quite sure that God is going to honor his prayer." I learned that the family shared, by mail, in the ministry of a preacher who taught a form of "prosperity theology." Our host gave me an audio cassette to which I listened when I returned to England. "Do you think God wants you to be poor?" the preacher asked. "Of course not. God wants to share His bounty with you. God wants you to prosper and succeed in your business. He wants you to enjoy wealth. Nothing is too much for God. Just ask in faith and it will be yours."

I listened with increasing discomfort. This seemed a cozy, self-centered view of Providence. It was far removed from the challenge of Jesus who had nowhere to lay his head and whose earthly reward was a cross. Who would not be willing to follow Him if it meant getting everything that was desired? Although that particular preacher is now deceased, this view of Providence persists.

The fundamental error in expecting God to deliver a flashy car lies in confusing wants and needs. They are far from the same. We *want* what we do not *need*—a better house, longer vacations, academically brilliant children, unrivaled popularity, success in our business—the list is endless. We *need* what we do not *want*. We *need* a larger concept of God, a wider vision of human need, growth in grace and holiness. "Oh God," we cry, "don't disturb me. Don't make me sort out my wants and my needs. Just satisfy my wants and leave me alone." God, however, like the eagle, insists on coming to disturb us.

The destruction of the nest by the parent eagles seems such a cruel act. But in apparent harshness is benevolent provision. The action of the parents is determined by the young eaglet's *needs* not by what its *wants*. Apply this to the working of divine providence and we begin to glimpse the awesome goodness of God. As we look back on our spiritual journey we can perhaps see how the Holy One was too gracious to give us what we asked for, giving us instead what we needed. At the time we were disappointed and disturbed. Now, looking back, we give thanks for God's provision.

The theological seminary where I studied had a tradition of sending out students in groups of six on a mission for the week before Palm Sunday. In my first year I was a member of a team assigned to a struggling rural area that embraced eight churches. During the week we held a morning Bible school for children, lunchtime meetings for the older members, and an evangelistic rally each evening. The eight congregations participated with great enthusiasm and it was an exhilarating experience for all of us.

Families from each of the churches shared in the hospitality arrangements. On arrival we were given a list of the homes to which all the team would go for evening meals. We quickly learned to look forward to those suppers! There was a friendly rivalry between the various churches and they vied with one another in feeding these hungry students. Each evening we were confronted with more food than even we could possibly manage—in every case, that is, except one.

The exception was unforgettable. On the Thursday evening we were scheduled to go to the home of a widower. Stanley was a quiet retired farm laborer, and was approaching his eightieth birthday. He was a faithful member of the smallest of the eight churches taking part in our mission. He was present at every service. Had you seen him in his well-worn shiny suit you would have assumed he was poor. By human standards he was. In God's account books, however, he was one of the richest men on earth. Stanley was a spiritual giant. In the prayer meetings before each evening service, his prayers were truly awesome. He was steeped in the Bible, the Methodist Hymnal, and *Pilgrim's Progress* and his language reflected it. That dear man had a spiritual stature and a natural grace that shone through everything he did. In a quite lovely way he was able to usher people into the presence of God. He was ruggedly sincere, nothing about him was trite or superficial. We theological students may have had much more formal knowledge than he, but alongside him we were still in the kindergarten of spiritual formation.

On the appointed day we found Stanley's little cottage with some difficulty. The village where he lived was not large but his tiny house was tucked away down a winding bridle path. There was a small patch of grass in front of the cottage and an old hawthorn hedge. As the six of us trooped through the garden gate he came to greet us. He led us into the cottage. The front door opened into a single downstairs room with a small kitchen off. In a corner of the room were some stairs that led to the only bedroom and a small bathroom. Everything spoke of poverty. The walls were covered in faded old wallpaper and on them were three pictures set in simple frames. One was of Stanley and his wife on their wedding day. Another was an old

Methodist favorite "Cornish Fishermen at Prayer." The third was a well-known picture of John Wesley preaching at a village cross.

We had been told that Stanley had no children. Sarah, his wife, had been his only love and she had died forty years earlier. We had wondered how he would cope with preparing a meal for six hungry students. The answer was waiting for us when we entered the house. The table was already laid. In a bowl were ten hard-boiled eggs. Beside it was a plate of sliced ham, a single large brown loaf, and a platter of butter. In the center of the table was a large jug of milk. Compared with the bounty we had experienced in the past few days this was frugal fare indeed. We concealed our disappointment. After all, we had been properly brought up and knew our manners. Trying to sound sincere we muttered appreciation at being in his home and took our places at the table. Our host bowed his head for grace. In his rich accent and with a voice pulsing with emotion Stanley whispered, "O Lord, we are so rich! Others are lost but we have been found. Others are brokenhearted but we are rejoicing. Others are friendless but we have each other. Others are hungry but we have eggs, meat, bread, butter and milk. Open our hearts to the needs of others as we give glory to you for your bounty, O most generous Lord. Amen."

I have sat at few tables so bountiful! It was unforgettable—and *disturbing*. Here was a man who could distinguish between wants and needs and recognized that what God gave was sufficient. This uneducated man through his simplicity was unconsciously teaching us a lesson about providential provision. Sitting around his table we learned that what we really needed was not yet another lavish meal but the kind of grace to become like this dear man of God.

Like the eagle, providence is disturbing in providing not for our wants but for our deepest needs.

PROVIDENCE—LIKE THE EAGLE—A DISTURBING STRIVER

The eaglets are thrust out of their nest. They stand shivering on the perilous ledge. Below are the threatening rocks. Above circle their parents who have not brought their offspring to this point to destroy them but to teach them to fly; to strive with them until they master the air. We can imagine the young ones asking themselves "Do we have to make the plunge? Why can't we be left in the nest? Do we have to be disturbed?"

Most of us have our own private fund of stories that we call providential. I think of a poor couple struggling to bring up a large family in a mining area. "I was unemployed," the man told me. "I had searched endlessly for work. We were down to our last penny and we simply did not know where the next meal was coming from. We took our need to God in prayer and, miraculously, an unexpected check arrived in the mail. It was providential."

"Our daughter was terribly ill," the mother told me after a service at a convention in England. "She had seen specialist after specialist. The doctors had given up hope and told us it was just a matter of time. The people at church began to pray for us. An all night vigil was held. Something wonderful happened; she turned the corner and lived. Today she is completely well. It was providential."

One day, when in family practice, I was driving down the road to my medical office. On impulse I stopped to call in on an elderly patient. When she opened the door she was amazed to see me. "Doctor!" she gasped. "How did you know?" "Know what?" I asked. She pointed to the rear room and said "I think my husband has just had a heart attack. I have already telephoned the emergency service." I had arrived at exactly the right moment and was able to offer immediate help. As I thought about it later I whispered to myself, "That was providential."

But then I think of other believing, struggling couples who receive no check. I know so many whose loved ones did not recover from a fatal illness despite much prayer. I had other patients on whom I did not feel led to call just as they were having a medical emergency. Where was providence in these cases? Are we to associate providence only with glad and successful experiences? Is God only God when things work out the way we want? Have we fixed our attention on the gift rather than the Giver?

There is no simple answer to these questions, and we must be cautious of anyone who claims to have one. The analogy of the eagle is helpful as we try to understand this mystery. God—the divine Author of every good and perfect gift—does not send pain or distress. He comes, however, to turn every hurdle into a stepping stone, every difficulty into an opportunity to grow. Left to ourselves we would prefer to curl up in the nest and nurse our hurts. God wants us out on the ledge stretching our wings so that we may fly.

When I was in the primary school there was a girl in my class who was unforgettable. Margaret had been born with a disfigurement that affected the whole of her left cheek. Despite what must have been a terrible handicap, she was the most popular child in the school, full of happiness and fun. At the age of ten I moved to another school, and she passed out of my life. Occasionally she would flit through my mind, and I wondered how she coped in the sensitive years of adolescence with such an embarrassing scar.

Years later, after entering the ministry, I was invited to preach at the anniversary of a Methodist church in my hometown. On arrival I was greeted by the church stewards. "Our Sunday School superintendent would like to have a word with you," one of them said. "I will go and fetch her." A minute or two later he returned accompanied by a young woman. It was Margaret! I recognized her immediately; the scar was impossible to conceal. She was radiant with an infectious smile and a delightful sense of humour. She had become one of the key leaders of that church.

Five years ago, I learned that Margaret had died of a cerebral tumor. Her husband brought me the news when I returned to my hometown on a preaching visit. He dissolved in tears at the church door as he told me of the desolation he had felt since her death. "It's been a year since she died," he told me, "but I still don't want to go back to the house. When I do, I sit at the foot of the stairs and cry." Then he added, "There was something quite wonderful about Margaret. When she gave her life to Christ as a teenager, it seemed as though God took her disfigurement and turned it into wings. Being married to her for thirty years was like being married to an angel."

"God took that disfigurement and turned it into wings." God did not send that disfigurement, and I am sure there were many times as she was growing up that Margaret begged for it to be taken away. God, however, did something better than simply removing the affliction. He transformed it into an instrument of spiritual growth and made her a shining inspiration to many. This is the marvellous work of providence. The ledge is intended to be a *launching* pad not a nesting place so that our souls may soar. God's ultimate plan is that our spirits should develop wings.

Like the eagle, providence is disturbing. It strives with us, turning our burdens into blessings.

PROVIDENCE—DISTURBING IN ITS SALVATION

All of us falter in our spiritual development. We are required to walk by faith, not by sight, and we stumble. Even the most stouthearted have dark nights of the spirit when faith seems to burn low. Few are spared times of doubt or discouragement and each of us has a personal share of pain. For one it is a doctor's report, for another the experience of love betrayed, for yet another uncertainty about the future. It is natural when discouraged to cry, "O God, why? Where is providence now?"

Look again at the eagle. As the helpless chicks fall, no match for the challenge to their immature strength, the mighty pinions of the parent eagle come underneath to bear them up. Here is a parable of providential care. God is saying "Go on! Step out in faith. Trust where you cannot trace. Throw yourself upon my mercy. Believe my promise that underneath are the everlasting arms." In an age looking for scientific evidence, we find it disturbing to rely on trust. This, however, is the way providence works. We cannot experience salvation until we have abandoned our reliance upon our own resources and have the courage to leap off the ledge into the arms of God.

I remember a preacher telling about a farmer's son named Joe who was seven years old. He was playing with his older friend Simon in a disused barn. They noticed a trapdoor in the boarded ceiling leading to the loft above. There was an old rickety ladder to the trapdoor. The loft used to be used for storing grain but had been empty for years. Intrigued the two boys climbed the ladder, undeterred by the complaining noises which it made, lifted the trapdoor and clambered up. There were windows on three of the walls of the loft and a large open space with a gantry on the fourth where, in former days, sacks of grain were lowered to wagons below. Although the windows were dirty, the loft was bathed in light. They had a great time examining some of the old equipment stored up there.

Eventually, it was time to go. Simon, the older boy, went down the ladder first. From years of disuse it had become rotten in parts and, after allowing the pair to climb up, now collapsed under the boy's weight coming down. He fell unharmed onto the straw below, but Joe was left stranded up in the loft. "Simon," Joe cried, "go and fetch dad." Simon ran to the farmhouse and brought Joe's father. The farmer came and stood beneath the open trapdoor. His boy was standing above him bathed in the light from the loft windows. The barn was in darkness. "Jump son," the farmer said. Joe was frightened and dazzled by the light of the loft. Below him was inky blackness. "Jump son," repeated the farmer, "I will catch you." "But daddy," Joe said, "I'm scared. I can't see you. I can't see anything down there." "Jump son," said his father. "Trust me. You may not be able to see me, but I can see you. Jump!"

Like the eagle, providence is disturbing in calling us to fling ourselves trustingly into the arms of God. It is a leap of faith, but that is the only way to find salvation.

Providence is not just another name for a snug, comfortable way out of all our problems when we are given special privileges and spared the slings and arrows of outrageous fortune. It is much better than that. God, like the eagle, provides for our real needs so that we can grow souls. God, like the eagle, strives with us and enables us to turn our handicaps and disappointments into wings. And then, when we have the courage to throw ourselves upon his goodness and mercy, like the eagle, He comes to bear us up on the mighty pinions of his infinate love and grace. It is disturbing, but then gloriously reassuring, to prove by experience that "the eternal God is our refuge and underneath are the everlasting arms." But first, we must jump!

But he replied to one of them,
"Friend, I am doing you no wrong;
Did you not agree with me for the usual daily wage?
Take what belongs to you and go;
I choose to give to this last the same as I give to you.
Am I not allowed to do what I choose
with what belongs to me?
Or are you envious because I am generous?"

MATTHEW 20:13–15 (NRSV)

Chapter Eleven

God's Accounting

August 1998

S ome years ago my wife and I took part in the pastoral exchange program between British and American Methodist churches. The church with which we were paired had two Sunday morning services, 8:30 and 11:00 A.M. I arrived for the early service on my first Sunday with some anxiety. I had not preached to a congregation in the United States before. The district superintendent was also nervous; he feared for both the preacher and the congregation and had kept the Sunday free so that he could be present and rescue the situation if necessary. We subsequently became good friends and for years afterwards we would recall our mutual trepidation with great amusement.

The singing at the first service was led by a men's chorus. At the appointed hour the district superintendent led me to the choir room where I was warmly welcomed. After he had prayed we processed into the sanctuary. One of the singers, a short, wiry man with an infectious chuckle in his voice, broke ranks as he passed and thrust a brown envelope into my hand. *"That's fun money,"* he whispered before scurrying back into line. I had not heard this expression before and naturally was puzzled. I put the envelope into my pocket and followed the choir into the sanctuary.

During the interval between the two services, I opened the envelope. In it were fifty crisp new one-dollar bills. I was bewildered and overwhelmed. I associated gifts with special occasions. I thought of them as tokens of esteem which had first to be earned. The brown envelope defied all the rules. It had been presented to me by a complete stranger. I had done absolutely nothing to deserve it. I had never laid eyes on him before that morning, and he had not heard me say a word. It seemed so very strange.

Later it dawned upon me that I was confusing rewards with gifts. The contents of the envelope were not intended as a reward which had been earned. They were a gift which expressed the nature of the generous giver. What I had experienced was *grace*.

All of us have our private collection of stories about the funny things children have said or done in public. My friend Derrick Greeves, a much loved British Methodist minister, told me of the appearance of his six-year-old granddaughter in a school nativity play. Hers was a minor part as an angel who uttered one line: *"Behold I bring you glad tidings of great joy."* She took her part very seriously and rehearsed again and again at home. She would stand at the top of the stairs declaiming, *"Behold I bring you glad tidings of great joy."* She would go into her parents' bedroom and stand on the dressing table stool so that she could see herself in the mirror. With arms outstretched, she would declare, *"Behold I bring you glad tidings of great joy."* Then she would gather a captive audience of parents and grandparents and hold forth, *"Behold I bring you glad tidings of great joy."*

The day of the performance arrived. Her parents and grandparents dutifully took their places and waited. Eventually she appeared on the platform, heavily disguised in makeup, walked slowly to the center of the stage and looked out at the audience. Then she froze! The audience waited and her family held their breath. After what seemed an eternity she spoke. In her panic, she stumbled over the first word and uttered what she so often heard mother say. In a loud voice she cried, *"Behave I bring you glad tidings of great joy."*

Her mistake is one we all make. We feel that we have to behave in order to receive good tidings. We find it difficult to accept the undeserved, free favor of God. Ours is a world of rewards rather than gifts and this is one reason why we have difficulty in grasping the good news which Jesus brings.

Most of us are familiar with the story of the rich young man who wanted to be a disciple. Recognizing that he was in bondage to his possessions, Jesus challenged him to let them go. This was too much for him and with a shake of the head he turned away. Watching his sorrowful departure, Jesus said "I tell you it is hard for a rich man to enter the kingdom of heaven." The disciples were dumbfounded. It was accepted wisdom that wealth, like health, was a sign of God's blessing. If a rich man were not able to enter the Kingdom, who on earth could? It was then that Peter spoke up. He said what they all were thinking. "We have left everything to follow you! What then will there be for us?" Since he and the other disciples had given up so much for the sake of the Kingdom, was it not reasonable to assume that they would be suitably rewarded?

Peter, like us, is essentially an accountant. Life for him has debit and credit columns. Here are two people. The first gives to God two hours of service, the second gives only one. It is simply basic, sound accounting to reward the first with double the wages of the second. Anything else would be unjust. When a person gives generously, works hard, serves sacrificially, then justice demands due recognition. It is against this background that Jesus tells the story of the laborers in the vineyard. The story is not about employment and contracts. It is not about terms and conditions of service. It is a message in code which lifts us above the world of rewards and wages to the realm of gifts. It is a story about the nature of grace and the gift of salvation. Its message is threefold.

A MESSAGE ABOUT THE DIVINE NATURE

I was deeply moved by the London production of the musical *Les Misérables*. It caused me to return to the novel by Victor Hugo on which it is based. This great story is not essentially about the squalid conditions of the poor but about the conflict between law and grace.

The central character is Jean Valjean. When we meet him he is being paroled from Toulon Prison after nineteen years of brutalizing treatment. Originally sentenced for stealing a loaf of bread, his term had been extended more than once because of attempts to escape. He is powerfully strong and has an unbreakable will. For four days after his release he wanders the village roads seeking shelter against the weather. Finally he knocks on the door of an old man whom the exconvict assumes to be the village priest. He is unaware that this is actually the residence of the Lord Bishop of Digne.

The saintly old bishop opens the door and is confronted by the burly, ugly, filthy and defiant figure of the paroled convict. Jean blurts out "I am Jean Valjean. I'm a convict on parole. I've done nineteen years in prison. I went to the inn and they turned me away. I tried the prison and the doorkeeper would not open to me. I crawled into a dog kennel and the dog bit me. I lay on a bench in the square and a good woman pointed to your house. I am tired and hungry. Will you let me stay?"

The bishop welcomes him in. "Sit down and warm yourself, Monsieur," he says. "Supper will soon be ready and the bed can be made up while you're having a meal." Jean is overwhelmed at being treated as a human being. He babbles like a child, "You really mean it? You will let me stay? You are calling me Monsieur?" The bishop lays his hand gently on Jean's arm. "This house is not mine but Christ's," he says. "It does not ask your name but whether you are in need. You are hungry and thirsty, and so you are welcome. This is more your home than mine. Everything in it is yours. You are my brother."

Sadly, the brutalizing years have seeped deep into Jean's soul. They have turned a harmless tree pruner into a hardened criminal. He rewards the kindness he has received by getting up in the middle of the night and making off with the bishop's silver. Next morning, shortly after the housekeeper has discovered the theft there is a commotion at the front door. Jean is standing there held by three gendarmes. They had found him with the silver and had immediately placed him under arrest. Now they have brought him together with the stolen goods to the bishop so that his crime can be confirmed. A word from the bishop and the ungrateful scoundrel will go back to jail for life. The doomed man waits to be denounced. To his utter amazement, however, the Bishop responds in a way he least expects. "So here you are," he cries to Valjean. "I'm delighted to see you. Had you forgotten that I gave you the candlesticks as well? They're silver like the rest, and worth a good 200 francs. Did you forget to take them?"

"My Lord," says the sergeant, "do I understand that this man was telling the truth?" Jean jerks up when he hears the words "My Lord." He is dumbfounded. "Do you mean to say he is not the local priest?" he asks. "Silence," thundered one of the gendarmes. "This is his lordship the Bishop." When the gendarmes have been dismissed, there follows the most moving moment in the whole novel, beautifully preserved in the modern musical production. The godly man hands the candlesticks to Jean and says: "Jean Valjean, my brother, you no longer belong to what is evil but to what is good. I have bought your soul to save it from black thoughts and the spirit of perdition, and I give it to God."

That does it! Jean is overwhelmed, and his life is changed. This act of the saintly bishop defies all logic. Pity might have caused him to help the convict in the first place but after his generosity is rewarded with such treacherous ingratitude Jean has surely forfeited any claim on his kindness. He *deserves* nothing. Justice demands he be taken back to Toulon jail to spend the rest of his life in chains. It is at this point, however, that the bishop, by his undeserved generosity, lifts us from the realm of justice to the realm of grace, which is the theme of the novel.

This story of laborers in the vineyard is first of all a message about God's nature. It directs our attention to his generous mercy, his grace. The laborers are not treated equally. Those who worked for one hour received the same wage as those who worked all day. It is not fair. Thank God, however, that in his dealings with us he is not fair. Were he to give us what we deserve would any of us be better off? Grace teaches us that we receive from God what we need and not what we deserve. This is what God is like. The laborer who spent most of the day waiting in the square had not earned a full days pay. He receives not what he has earned but what he and his family need. The story gives a glimpse into the heart of God, the author of grace.

A MESSAGE ABOUT HUMAN NATURE

In the story, Jesus is talking about the lowliest men in Palestinian society—the day laborers. These men would sometimes envy the slaves and servants of the great house because what these others lacked in freedom they made up for in security. The day laborers were free. That was about the only good thing which could be said about them. But freedom was not much comfort when the larder was empty and the children were crying for bread. Each day these men would get up before dawn, take their tools and their lunch and stand in the marketplace in the hope of being hired from 6:00 A.M. until 6:00 P.M. If lucky, they might be offered work. The going rate for a full day's labor was a denarius, just enough to provide survival food for a family. For these laborers life was always grim, hovering around the starvation line. Unemployment even for a few days was not just unfortunate, it was a disaster.

Let us slip into the market square as dawn breaks and follow the fortunes of one of these laborers. It is the time of the grape harvest when the demand for labor is unpredictable. The owner of a vineyard arrives wanting, let's say, ten workers. See how the laborer stands on tiptoe, his hopes rising as men are chosen. Then his hopes are dashed when he is left behind. He waits for another opportunity. His emotions are on a roller coaster as on three more occasions, at 9:00 A.M., noon, and 3:00 P.M. the owner of the vineyard returns to take on more men. On each occasion he is passed over. The day wears on but, do you notice, he stays. He clings to the slim hope that the owner may yet return for more help. The sun is moving towards the west and the laborer's hope is ebbing away. The prospect of returning empty-handed to a hungry family stares him in the face.

And then it happens! At 5:00 P.M. the owner returns to the market square and says, "I want you also to go and work in my vineyard."

Consider two pictures of this man. The first is when he is standing in the market square hoping to find work. Can you see how miserable and dejected he looks? Do you see the futility written across his face? Can you hear him asking himself "What am I here for? Does life have any meaning?" Now look at the second picture when he is working in the vineyard. Do you see the transformation? He is stripped to the waist. Sweat pours down his face as he heaves the great baskets of grapes onto his back. But look at his face. Do you see that sparkle in his eye? Can't you hear him singing as he works? He is not asking what the purpose in life is now. He feels that he belongs.

During the nights of bombing in the Second World War, I recall as a child going into the air raid shelter with the rest of my family. Dad would bring out a jigsaw puzzle. By the light of a dim kerosene lamp he would mix up the pieces on the small table and then assign parts to each of his five children. The puzzle was, perhaps, a hunting scene. "Doreen," he would say to my sister, "I want you to do the edges. George, you do the trees. Rex you do the dogs. Ron you do the horses. Reg you do the sky." I hated doing the sky! Piece after piece of blue! It was hard and boring. Eventually it would be finished and soon afterwards we would hear the sirens sounding the "all clear" which meant that we could return to our home. Dad's purpose in taking our minds off the bombing, had been accomplished. And then we would, perhaps, find that a piece was missing. So often it was a piece of sky. Suddenly an insignificant piece of blue became the most important part of the puzzle because without it the picture was incomplete. This is the story of our lives. Seen in isolation, in the marketplace, against the background of this world, they seem meaningless. But seen in the context of God's purposes they become robed with significance as they complete His grand design. That is where we belong and without us the plan of God is incomplete.

Imagine an intelligent alien visiting a circus. He might understand the movements of the horses, the lions, and the trapeze artists. He would, perhaps, see how form and function blend perfectly together, how muscle, sinew, and training resulted in splendidly coordinated movements. He would, however, be baffled by the performing seals, always a special feature in the shows of my childhood. They sit in the circus ring so gracefully, balancing large beach balls on their noses and tossing them to one another. But then when they walk there is nothing graceful about their movements whatsoever. They look almost ridiculous as they waddle in the most ungainly fashion, their flippers so unsuitable for motion. These beautiful shapely creatures look frankly absurd. Our intelligent alien is bewildered. This does not make sense. He sees a fundamental contradiction between their streamlined bodies and their absurd gait.

But later he sees the seals in the lake where they live. He sees them diving and gliding through the water with grace and ease. And now the light dawns. Of course! These handsome creatures were not made for land. They were created for the water and only there do they make sense.

Just as the laborer does not rise to his full significance until he moves from the market place to the vineyard, so we do not reach our full stature until we find our place in the Kingdom of God and within the divine will and purpose. This is beautifully expressed in the words of St. Augustine; "Thou hast made us for Thyself and our hearts are restless until they rest in Thee." Our nature cannot be explained in terms of biology and physiology. There is a fundamental mystery and contradiction about us until we are set in the context of eternity. We are made for God.

A Message about the Nature of Salvation

I had just passed my seventh birthday when I saw a toy car in the cycle shop owned by Mr. Jones. It was a case of love at first sight. The object of my desire was a blue Mercedes. I had to pass the shop on my way home from school and church, and the more I saw it, the more I longed to have it. Its price ticket read one shilling and six pence—eighteen pence, a fortune! I would stand gazing at the car through the window with my nose pressed against the glass, dreaming of owning it. This was serious business, and so one day I discussed the matter with the wisest and kindest person in the whole world—my mother. She said, "Why don't you join Mr. Jones's Christmas Club and have it put by so that you can save up for it out of your pocket money?" The more I thought about it, the more I felt that this made good sense. I made the decision. Yes, I would join the Christmas Club.

The following Saturday when we received our weekly pocket money of two pence, I set off for the cycle shop. Two of my brothers, intrigued by my resolve, went with me to watch the spectacle as I joined the Christmas Club. With all the solemnity of preparing a mortgage document, Mr. Jones made out a Christmas Club Subscription Card. He checked the calendar and explained that he would put my name beside the car. If I paid a penny a week it would become mine on the Saturday before Christmas. I duly paid my first penny, received the card and took it home to my mother. She carefully put it behind the clock on the mantel—the place where all our family's important documents such as school report cards were placed. Each week I would carry the card back to the shop, hand over a penny, see it entered on the record and then make sure the card was returned to its place of safety.

Eventually the day came when I paid in the last penny and Mr. Jones made the final entry. Solemnly he wrote across the card the wonderful words "Paid In Full" and added his signature. Then he handed the blue car to me. At long last it was mine! Triumphantly I carried it home. It was the first time I had ever conducted such a major transaction.

It is a common fallacy amongst Christians to think of eternal life and salvation like Mr. Jones's Christmas Club. We solemnly present our weekly penny—our time, our love, our labor, our prayers, our worship. Subconsciously, we think of these being entered onto a contributions card and think that one day the card will be handed in and we will receive in exchange something we call "salvation."

This is human accountancy. It is the kind of mathematics of which Simon Peter was thinking when he made his statement that caused Jesus to tell the story of the laborers in the vineyard. It is so easy to think that if we build up a balance of goodness, love, kindness, and mercy we will eventually have enough on the card to merit eternal life. We are bound to the concept of earning and receiving rewards and wages. In this story Jesus is telling us to move from the realm of reward to the realm of gift. Salvation is not earned. It is not a wage. It is a gift out of God's undeserved love. It is grace.

Best of all, it does not begin when we leave this life. It begins now. Working in the vineyard, joining in the purposes of God by sharing in the work of the Kingdom here in the place where we live and love and laugh and work, this is salvation.

One day Jesus was praying
in a certain place. When he finished,
one of his disciples said to him,
"Lord, teach us to pray,
just as John taught his disciples."
He said to them, "When you pray, say:
'Father, hallowed be your name, . . .'"

LUKE 11:1–2 (NIV)

Chapter Twelve

The Language of Love

August 1991

*E*very Tuesday morning during my years in Manchester I attended an area planning meeting at the Methodist headquarters that were at the heart of the city's commercial center. Between the headquarters and the church which I served lay half a mile of some of the busiest streets in England. It did not take me long to discover that the quickest and most convenient means of getting around in that part of Manchester was by walking. Leaving the quiet retreat of my study and threading my way on foot through the busy, noisy traffic was not the most soothing of experiences.

One day a friend introduced me to a secret concealed just a few hundred yards from my office. Tucked out of sight in a little side street was the lovely Catholic church of Saint Mary. I had walked past that street many a time and not seen it because it was hidden by tall office buildings. My friend told me that it was affectionately known as "The Hidden Gem." The moment I entered, I experienced a thrilling sense of God's presence. In that sacred place was a holy quiet. From then on, each Tuesday, I would leave my office early so that I could slip in and spend some time there. On every occasion I found an overwhelming inner peace and tranquillity. It was a glimpse of heaven. I often reflected as I sat in that lovely sanctuary that, although the "Gem" was hidden from the obvious notice of the city, without it the city and all its commerce were meaningless.

Each of us needs such a personal hidden gem at the center of our lives, a place of inner quiet where we can be still and recognize the presence of God. This is what prayer is. It is an inner house of quiet where our souls develop. It is the indispensable factor for spiritual growth. It is possible to have a deep life in the spirit without profound scholarship; after all, some great saints have lacked learning. This is not true of prayer; it is simply impossible to live the spiritual life without it.

Shortly after the evacuation of the British expeditionary force from Dunkirk in 1940, it is said that there was a rush to commission a whole new intake of officers. One of these, a raw nervous second lieutenant, was learning how to drill a squad of recruits under the eagle eye of the regimental sergeant major. The battalion was billeted on the south coast of England just outside Eastbourne. The inexperienced officer had his men marching towards the chalk cliffs of Beachy Head, a familiar sight for tourists where the coast of Sussex meets the English Channel with a five-hundred-foot sheer drop. The officer intended to give the command "about turn." Unfortunately, at that precise moment, he was overcome with nervousness, and he just stood and stuttered. Except for the sergeant major, the members of the squad were unaware that they were heading for the edge of the cliff and impending disaster. As the officer tried to find the right words the sergeant major called out "Say something, Sir, even if it's only 'goodbye.'"

Prayer is not a matter of mere words; it is not just "saying something." It is a vital and fundamental part of the spiritual life, an expression of a personal relationship with God. Luke tells us that the disciples stumbled upon Jesus after he had slipped away and was praying in a solitary place. Of course they were no strangers to the practice of prayer. After all, they attended the synagogue and the temple as well as observing the Sabbath. Prayers played an important part in each of these activities. But as they watched Jesus at prayer they realized they had encountered something altogether unique. It was not so much the words he used but rather his whole attitude towards God which was so different. He seemed to be on such amazingly familiar terms with the Almighty.

The church never forgot that when Jesus was laying his soul out to God in the extremity of his inner anguish in Gethsemane, he summed up his relationship by crying "abba." This was not simply "father." It was much more familiar than that. Perhaps the first word a Hebrew child uttered would be "abba"—daddy. To this day one of the first words children in that part of the world say is "jaba," and that means the same. We must not overlook how revolutionary this was. I remember one of my seminary teachers telling us that Professor Jeremias, one of the greatest New Testament scholars of the past one hundred years, said there is no parallel in the whole of Jewish literature to such a familiar approach to God. What the disciples witnessed when they saw Jesus at prayer so awed them that they gasped "Lord, teach us to pray!"

The meaning of prayer for Jesus did not lie just in words but in an attitude of mind and heart toward God which permeated the whole of his life. It was an attitude derived from love and devotion and summed up in four words: "hallowed be Thy name."

PRAYER MEANS HALLOWING GOD WITH OUR MINDS—
MORAL INTEGRITY

When God is hallowed in our minds, then our prayer becomes honest. It has the clothes of sincerity.

Some years ago my wife and I had the privilege of being taken by mutual friends to visit Billy and Ruth Graham at their home in Montreat, North Carolina. During our visit Billy told us a number of fascinating stories. One was of an incident when he was flying on a jet from New York to North Carolina. He said that an overweight drunken man boarded the plane. The flight attendants could not find a seat big enough for him, so they had to pull out a middle partition and he occupied two seats. He was cursing all the time and after a while, having tried in vain to flirt with the flight attendants, he decided to go and help the pilot fly the plane. Finally the flight attendant had to call the copilot, a large muscular man. He came and "persuaded" this man to return to his seat. Just then someone whispered that Billy Graham was sitting behind him. He got up, turned round and said, "Are you Billy Graham?" Billy nodded and the man said, "Then I want to shake your hand, your sermons have done me a power of good." Billy laughed and added to us, "I think he felt that he had to say something and those were the first words that came into his mind."

As we enjoyed the story, I could not help contrasting in my mind the thoughtless words of that intoxicated man and the shining integrity of Billy Graham who for half a century has championed the cause of evangelism. Words can be cheap, integrity is always costly. It is easy to talk about prayer. It is easy to throw in the phrase "I'll keep you in my prayers," but do those words reach down to the depth of our being? Do they enter the inner sanctuary where we make our decisions and determine our priorities? The language of love is the language of moral integrity.

In every church in British Methodism there is a room called the vestry. Here the preacher robes and prepares himself quietly for worship. Just before the service begins it is the tradition for one of the lay church stewards to pray with and for the minister. In my first appointment, on my very first Sunday morning, I arrived at the church early, nervous and apprehensive. I had approached the Sunday with trepidation having worked hard on the sermon. I lost count of the number of times I had read and reread the manuscript. Now the day had dawned, and here I was in the vestry, waiting for the stewards, my mind filled with the sermon.

Five minutes before the appointed hour of the service, I heard the footsteps of the three church stewards as they came down the corridor. I turned to face them as they entered. They were led by George, a distinguished looking eighty-six-year-old lifelong member of that church. They gathered around the table and then fell to their knees. I joined them as George prayed. And how he prayed! I had never heard anything like it. None of us in that room was aware that George had been told he had only weeks to live. At one point I happened to glance at him and was powerfully moved by his radiant face and the sight of the tears on his cheeks as he prayed. I can only describe his attitude as one of holy awe. He expressed in his prayer a sense of wonder and privilege that we mere mortals were to be allowed to do business with the Holy One who inhabited the heavens. He seemed to have entered another world and was transfigured in our presence by his deep sincere reverence. Then in his prayer he mentioned my name and the worship I was about to lead. He made me aware of the fearful responsibility that was mine. My eyes were lifted from my carefully prepared sermon to the awesome holiness of God and the moral integrity which God required. George opened my eyes to see that a sermon is not just words, it is a preacher's life which communicates to the worshippers.

A few weeks later we held George's funeral service, and as we sang the hymns he had chosen, I was taken back to that transcendental moment in the vestry on my first Sunday morning. There was a complete absence of pretense about this saintly man. He loved God with all of his mind, and his prayer was more than words; it was an expression of a life lived in the heavenly places. His prayer was robed in the clothes of sincerity and integrity.

Hallowed be Thy name *in my mind.*

PRAYER MEANS HALLOWING GOD WITH OUR HEARTS—
PASSIONATE PRAYER

Some years ago there was a popular radio personality in Britain named David Franklin. He had been a promising baritone singer but surgery on his vocal cords had halted his singing career. David Franklin took part in many musical quiz shows. On one occasion I heard him recalling some of his early experiences as a singer. The interviewer asked him if there was any particular person who had influenced him. Without hesitation he said, "Yes, Heddle Nash." Nash was one of the most sought after tenors in the country at that time. Choral societies would vie with one another to secure him whenever a great choral work was to be performed.

David Franklin told of his admiration for Nash and said that perhaps the quality which stood out above all others was the passion which he brought to his singing. He illustrated it by telling of an experience he once had in a concert with another tenor who was the exact opposite. The occasion was the first time that Franklin had ever sung in a performance of Verdi's "Requiem." He arrived at the concert hall early and sat in the dressing room reserved for the lead singers. He told us how excited and terrified he was as he sat there clutching the musical score, his mind totally taken up with what he was about to sing. Then the door opened and in stormed the leading tenor. He took his coat off, flung his score on the table and said disparagingly, "Another wretched requiem, but I suppose I have to do it. It's one way to earn a living." Then he sank into an armchair. David Franklin said, "I was shattered. There was no sense of excitement in this man's attitude. There was no joy, no exhilaration, no passion. For him, it was just a duty. He was doing something because he was paid for it."

Franklin went on to say, "Heddle Nash was as far removed from the attitude of that tenor as night is from day. For Nash no performance was a duty; it was always a labor of love. Every appearance he made on the concert stage was filled with passion. Whenever he took part in any choral work you would think it was his first and his last performance. He put his whole heart into it."

Similarly, prayer must be for us a matter of love and passion rather than duty. We must be careful not to belittle duty. We have a duty to come to worship. We have a duty to support God's work with our offerings and with our lives. We have a duty to offer God worship and prayer. But is it enough to do these things purely from duty?

We look for more than duty in our human relationships. Suppose a man remembers his wife's birthday, goes to the florist and buys a lovely floral arrangement. I wonder what would happen if he were to take those flowers home, but before handing them to his delighted wife he were to say, "Darling, today is your birthday. For fifteen years we have been married, and you have cooked my meals, washed and ironed my shirts, and kept house beautifully. I am very grateful for all this and I realize that as a consequence I have certain responsibilities and duties. One of these is my duty to observe special occasions. Today is your birthday. I made a note of it so that I would honor my responsibility. I want you to have these flowers as the fulfillment of my obligation and duty." I would not be surprised if his wife felt inclined to wrap those flowers around his smug neck. Duty indeed! What about love? What about passion?

There is magic in the word *love* because it brings with it *delight*. The psalmist sees obedience to the will of God not in terms of duty but in terms of love:

> *. . . for I delight in your commands*
> *because I love them.*
> *I lift up my hands to your commands*
> *which I love,*
> *and I meditate on your decrees* (Ps. 119:47–48 [NIV]).

Like most preachers, I have visited some churches where things appear on the surface to be mildly chaotic but I find my heart giving a leap as I go there. Why? Because I know that love radiates from the congregation. The members have gathered not out of a sense of duty but out of a sense of eager anticipation. As a result the service takes wings. Where Christ is adored passionately it doesn't matter if things go a little awry.

Prayer is not the language of duty it is the language of the heart, of loving adoration.

Hallowed be Thy name *in my heart!*

PRAYER MEANS HALLOWING GOD WITH OUR HANDS— COMMITTED PRAYER

A favorite book of former generations in England was *Tom Brown's School Days*. The author, a judge, published the book in 1857 little realizing that it would go through over sixty editions and be read around the world. In its way, it is a classic. Essentially a story about boys and their escapades, it gives a faithful picture of the changes that were taking place in English private boarding schools in the nineteenth century. The story is about the famous and historic Rugby School. It describes the influence of one of the most outstanding reformers in education, Dr. Thomas Arnold. Arnold, a devout clergyman became the headmaster of Rugby School at the age of thirty-two. He was a commanding figure who left an indelible mark upon the education system of his day and cast a spell for good on the character of every boy in his charge.

One day a weak, frightened boy named Arthur is brought to Rugby School by his anxious mother. Arthur's father is dead, and mother and son have been drawn very close to one another. He is a slight, pale delicate child, a quivering little bundle of nerves. Dr. Arnold gives Tom Brown the responsibility of looking after the novice and guarding him from the school bullies. The scared newcomer is not sure of himself. He is continually asking Brown's permission before he does anything. "Please Brown may I do this . . . may I do that." "Please Brown, may I wash my hands?" But that night in the dormitory where there were twelve loud and rough boys, Arthur does something for which he does not ask permission. Tom Brown is not looking when he hears jeers coming from some of the other boys in the dormitory. He turns round and sees the reason. Arthur has knelt by his bed in full view of the others to say his evening prayers.

Later that night Tom Brown lies in bed thinking of his own mother, and the prayers that she had taught him to say at her knee. He remembers how he had promised her that wherever he was, he would never go to bed before saying those prayers. Then he recalls how he did not have the courage to keep that promise when he came to Rugby School. He had been a coward, afraid of what the other boys would think. Now this delicate little newcomer has shamed him by nailing his colors to the mast. Then and there he makes a decision. Next morning, he kneels beside his bed and mutters, "God be merciful to me a sinner." Subsequently, others in the dormitory follow suit. Arthur, the fragile tadpole, in spite of ridicule, was prepared to hallow the name of God by what he did and this eventually earned the respect of his mockers.

Prayer is more than words. Prayer is expressed in the work of our hands and the activities of our lives.

In common with all the men of my generation, graduation from adolescence to adulthood was punctuated by a period of compulsory military service. The training battalion or boot camp experience is a sharp learning curve. For those such as I who had a quite sheltered upbringing it came as a jolt to be introduced to a uniform that did not fit, a haircut which was not wanted, and language not heard before. I was in a unit with twenty-nine others; most of them were rough, blaspheming, and apparently godless. On the first day we were assembled outside the barrack block to meet the drill corporal. There was a good deal of bravado and swaggering from some of the group who thought this was all some sort of game.

Then the corporal arrived. He was a muscular, rugged, seasoned campaigner from World War II with two rows of ribbons on his chest. His very presence was intimidating. He barked the speech that he gave to all new recruits explaining that he and the sergeant were going to turn us into something resembling soldiers in the following four weeks. We were left in no doubt that he considered us a pathetic unpromising bunch but that he intended to introduce some changes. "No intake, no matter how hopeless, has ever defeated me," he said. "And I do not intend to spoil that record." There was no swaggering by the time he had finished. We were impressed and subdued.

At the end of that first day, I was sitting on the edge of my bed writing a letter just before lights out. Then I noticed that suddenly the conversation around me stopped. I looked up and saw what had caused the hush. The corporal's bed was at the far end of the unit, in a commanding position. This tough professional soldier was on his knees at the bedside saying his prayers. I don't know how that affected the other men but I know how it impressed me. Unashamedly, he was acknowledging that he honored God by what he did.

Hallowed be thy name in my life, *with my hands.*

Oh, dear God, may my prayer be the language of the love that comes through the refining fire of my mind so that it has intellectual and moral integrity. May my prayer be the language of the love that comes not from a sense of duty, but from the passion of my heart. May my prayer be the language of love that comes from the actions of my will and the work of my hands in what I do. For your mercy's sake! Amen.

$\mathcal{N}otes$

CHAPTER 3

1. A. A. Milne, "Now We Are Six" (n.p.: Methmen Children's Books, n.d.) 102.

CHAPTER 6

1. J. Wallace Hamilton, "Overwhelmed" (n.p.: Spiritual Life Publishers, 1968) 31.

CHAPTER 7

1. Zan W. Holmes Jr., *Encountering Jesus* (Nashville: Abingdon Press, 1992) 68.

2. Charles Reid, *Malcolm Sargent: A Biography by Charles Reid* (London: Hodder and Stoughton, 1968) xv.

3. Charles R. Swindoll, *Laugh Again* (Nashville: Word Publishing, 1992) quoting from *The Window and Other Essays* (Boise: Pacific Press Publishing Association, 1973) 5–7.

CHAPTER 8

1. Swindoll, *Simple Faith* (Nashville: Word Publishing, 1991) 95.

About the Author

✝

Dr. Reginald Mallett is both an ordained British Methodist minister and a physician. He studied theology at the University of London and medicine at the University of Birmingham, England.

In medicine, he has held senior positions in the British Health Service. In ministry, he has preached extensively in Britain and the United States. For the past thirty-five years, he has been a speaker at many gatherings at Lake Junaluska. He is the author of *God's Coming in Christ, Journeying with Jesus*, and *The Cradle and the Star*. He and his wife, Brenda, have two children and five grandchildren.